Peeling

Black radish

Butternut squash

Aubergine (eggplant)

Salsify

Carrots

Kohlrabi

Asparagus

Pumpkin

Courgette (zucchini)

Beetroot (beet)

Sweet potato

FRITES

Anne de la Forest

FRITES

Photography **Guillaume Czerw**
Styling **Sophie Dupuis-Gaulier**
Illustrations and graphics
Le Bureau Des Affaires Graphiques

jacqui small

CONTENTS

FETA FRITES

Polenta frites

Pain perdu frites

PANISSE FRITES

Parsnip frites

Carrot frites

Beetroot (beet) frites

COMTÉ CHEESE FRITES

Green pea frites

POMMES PAILLES

Pear frites

Aubergine (eggplant) frites

THYME AND PARMESAN FRITES

INTRODUCTION

By Anne de la Forest

"It would be cruel to take away from our children the one thing that sweetens a long day's study. If they cannot look forward to a good plate of frites, how can they properly swallow physics and chemistry or digest biology?"

Patrick Besson, *Le Point*, November 2011

It was while enjoying a plate of frites that the idea for this book came to me ... four years ago.

I was savouring these little fried potato delicacies, remembering family lunches where the dish sat proudly at the centre of the table... We had to wait patiently until everyone was served with roast beef before we could attack the plate of crispy frites with a fork, which I would take straight to my mouth without even passing by my plate. And as soon as my mother turned her back, I'd steal them with my fingers! No ketchup or mayonnaise in those days... just generously salted and fried as they should be. The unforgettable taste of frites is lodged in all our minds, conjuring up intense and nostalgic memories of our childhood.

The history of this dish, popular worldwide, lies firmly in France... Despite the Belgians appropriating it as their national dish, frites originated in Paris.

France, renowned for her gastronomic talent, is responsible for making frites famous and exporting them around the world.

The Belgians, the Brits and the Americans have succeeded in making their own culinary history with their *baraque à frites*, their chip shops and their somewhat appropriately named French fries.

And what about you? What is your emotional connection to this dish? Were you the child who jumped for joy when he discovered frites were on the school menu? Or the employee who protested with colleagues when the staff canteen announced no more frites[1]? Would you frequent the Paris restaurant[2] whose reputation hung on its frites served exclusively on Thursdays... or are you simply the steadfast gourmet who wants to know how to make really good frites at home?

Frites are something of a culinary icon, bringing joy to people of all generations and backgrounds for the duration of a meal... so let us enjoy.

[1] A story recounted by the head of the workers council of the SNCF in Paris

[2] The restaurant *Nénesse*, 17 rue de Saintonge, Paris

Note for readers: Due to the different names given to fried potatoes in different parts of the world, unless we are specifically referring to American 'French fries' or English 'chips', we use the term 'frites' to refer to fried potatoes and other fried vegetables and fruits in the recipes in this book.

LONG LIVE THE FRITE! LONG LIVE CHEMISTRY!

By Hervé This

What does chemistry have to do with the story of frites? Well, if we take the definition of chemistry as a scientific activity that tries to discover the causes of various pheonmena, then we can apply scientific principles to the science behind cooking the perfect frite.

Chemistry is used in many other applications outside of the laboratory: food, cosmetics, paint, varnish, candles, medication... although not considered purely scientific, their manufacture uses the art of chemistry to create different products. So, why not use chemistry to understand the science in our kitchens ?

And the frite in all this? The frite, or rather the making of the frite, reveals many extraordinary chemical phenomena: the bubbling of the oil as the frites are lowered into it, the white smoke that fills the pan; the formation of a crust around the frite, the browning of the surface... Fully understanding how a frite is formed is a scientific process.

Couldn't we simply make frites as we always have, by throwing sticks of potato into hot oil? Yes, but the issue is how to make perfect frites. And the idea of throwing potatoes into hot oil is all very well but begs a million questions: What size stick? Which type of potato? What age of potato? How should the sticks be cut? How should they be kept? What kind of oil should you use? How hot should it be? How often can you re-use it? How many times should you cook the frites? How long for each time?

Faced with such questions, the technician's only recourse is to carry out repeated experiments... and to use a strict methodology...

As far as frites are concerned, allow me to draw on numerous experiments. Everything has been examined; most notably the temperature and the pressure of the frite at the moment of frying. This may sound slightly crazy but just wait – the results speak for themselves!

Is the frite surrounded by bubbles as you throw it into the oil? Yes, because the heat of the oil causes the water to evaporate. Does this water evaporate from the vegetable's flesh? Yes, 1 ml (0.03 fl oz) of water creates approximately 1 litre (1 quart) of steam, which is what causes these numerous bubbles. So, is it the vegetable that causes these bubbles? Yes, because the little sticks of potato cannot contain this large volume of steam. So the steam escapes? Yes, because the pressure increases. If you look closely, you can see tiny jets of steam escaping.

You see, there was a clear logic to measuring the pressure in the frite... and expectations were not disappointed. After a few minor burns, the results are there: when you place a frite in hot oil, the pressure inside slowly starts to rise; then, as you remove it from the oil, the pressure will continue to rise slightly, before falling.

What is the purpose of all this? To find out, among other things, how many times you should cook your frites. In fact, the finding of the experiment just described is that, when the frite is removed from the oil, its surface is covered with fat. The potato absorbs the oil when the pressure decreases, due to the condensation of the steam. If you cook the frite once only, it has only one coating of fat. If you cook it twice, it has two.

A few statistics help to illustrate this theory: if we start with 100 grams (3½ oz) of frites, which we drop into the deep fryer and if, when we lift them from the fryer, we carefully dry the surface of the frite, we can avoid the absorption of 1 tablespoon of oil.

So, wasn't the short chemistry lesson worth it?

To conclude, I think that the art of cooking is greatly embellished once you understand that the technique is not complicated, and that cooking is first of all about love and then about art.

So, should your frites be golden or simply yellow? Now that is a question of personal taste, a question of aesthetics... nothing to do with technique.

To fully understand this question it's worth comparing it to a question about painting. In painting, you have to first distinguish between the painter and the artist. Both use paints and brushes, but their objective is not necessarily the same: the first aims to cover walls and to protect them, the second aims to leave an impression. In cooking, and especially in the preparation of frites, the same holds true: every good cook has the technique but some are craftsmen whilst others are artists. The chef who serves frites simply to feed a hungry table is a craftsman. But the chef who uses a dish of frites as a base for 'spiritual communion' is an artist.

Remember, the first principle of good cooking is not art but love; or should we say, human interaction. How can I best explain this? The tastiest dishes, a dish created by the most renowned artist, will never be good if it is simply served up for the guests. On the other hand, if the cook has created his dish of frites with genuine love, then the simple frite will achieve perfection.

Let's learn to say 'I love you'.

Hervé This is the co-author of *Molecular Gastronomy*. He is an INRA chemist (the National Institute for Agronomic Research), professor of AgroParisTech, and scientific director of the **Foundation of Food Science and Culture**.

http://hervethis.blogspot.com/

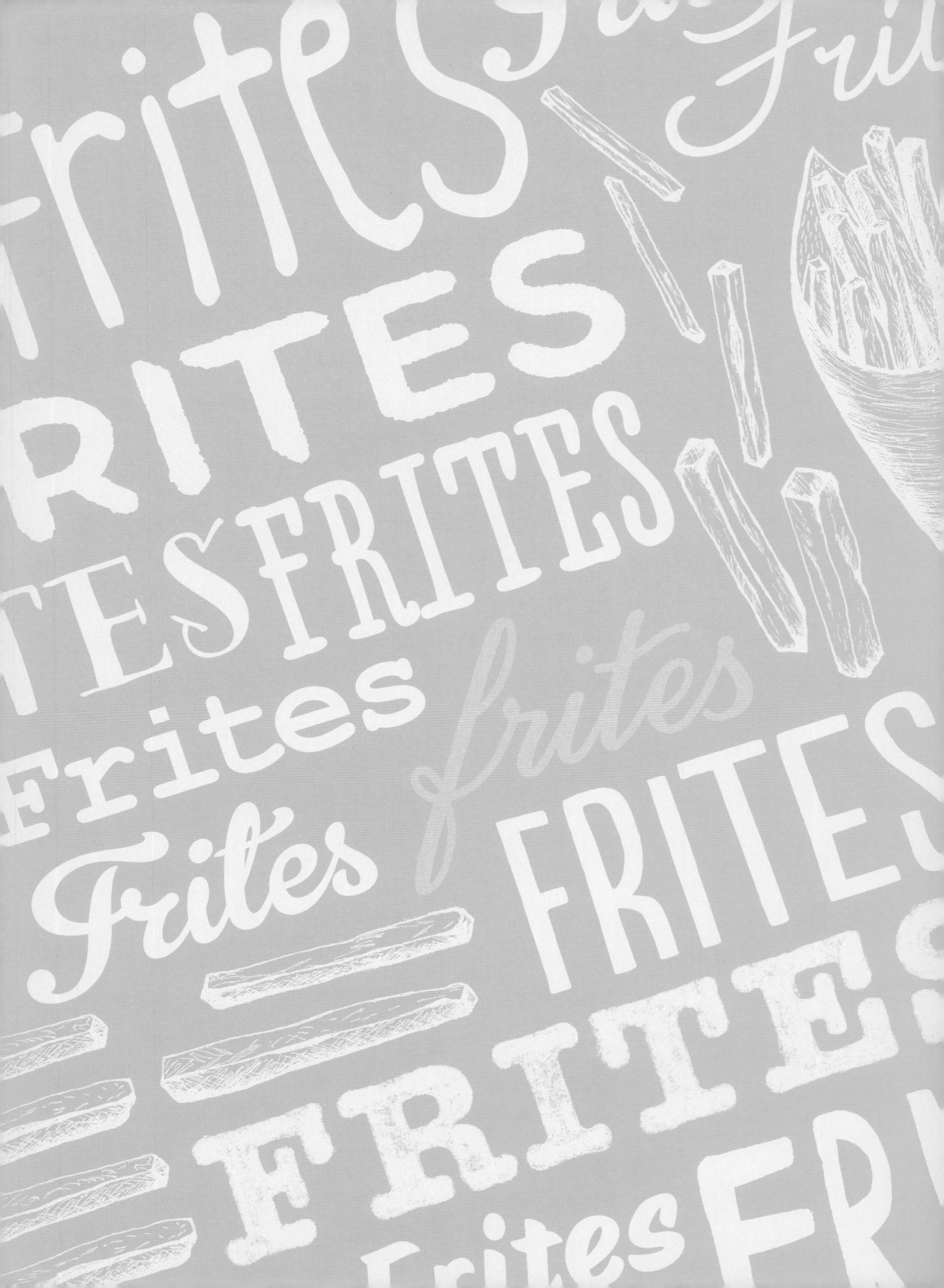
FRITES
FRITES
Frites
Frites
frites
FRITES
FRITES

Frites

The epic tale
of the frite

FRITES

FRITES

ES FRITES

Frites Frite

THE EPIC TALE OF THE FRITE

What a subject !

Considering that frites are a food that people worldwide associate with emotion and nostalgia, establishing their origin is a thorny issue with both specialists and patriots. For years the French and the Belgians have been battling it out with research, demonstrations and contradictory articles[2] – each trying to prove, of course, that the dish is their own. By carrying out my own research (and I am no historian but simply a food enthusiast) and encountering various passionate gastronomes[3] along the way, I have been unable to reach a definitive conclusion. However, when the UN declared 2008 to be the Year of the Potato, a number of universities dedicated themselves to the subject and one very complete work[4] was published in France, that shed some light on the issue. I was reassured to discover two entire chapters dedicated to *la frite*. It was something of a relief. Belgium has built a large part of her popular history on this dish, which is inseparably linked to the famous *baraque à frites* (street stalls selling frites), and Belgian enthusiasts and local historians have not hesitated to dig deeper into the subject to prove their country's pre-eminence. But there is no clear proof that they were the inventors, as they claim, of this fried potato stick. Without going to quite such lengths, no doubt reassured by her superior culinary reputation and content in the knowledge that the Anglo-Saxons talk about *French* fries, France has always claimed ownership of the frite for herself.

> ## " Without doubt, a frite gastronomy exists, and we should look carefully at the arguments of the purists "
>
> Jean-Paul Barrière[1].

1 Professor of Contemporary History, IRHiS, Université Charles-de-Gaulle Lille 3, *La pomme de terre de la renaissance au XXI^{e}s,* éd. Presses Universitaires François Rabelais, p.226

2 www.frites.be/; www.musee-gourmandise.be/

3 Thanks to Christian Dubois, enthusiast and member of the Académie Culinaire, for his help (cuisine.passion.blog.com)

4 *La pomme de terre de la renaissance au XXI^{e}s,* éd. Presses Universitaires François Rabelais

5 In 1789, Antoine-Auguste Parmentier published a treatise on the cultivation and uses of the potato, sweet potato and Jerusalem arthichoke

Thank you
Monsieur Parmentier

Grown today in more than 100 countries, the potato is truly a universal product. The *papa*, as it was called nearly 1,000 years ago, first appeared in the Andean mountains (Peru, Bolivia and Chile all claim ownership) but didn't arrive in France until the 16th century when the Spanish introduced it to Europe. A rather unattractive tuber, grown by germination (as opposed to plantation), resistant to harsh climates, tasteless, starchy and accused of causing numerous illnesses and of draining the soil of nutrients... the potato wasn't really a big hit initially with the French and when production of it was permitted, it was used for animal feed. It is thanks to the pharmacist and food hygienist Antoine-Auguste Parmentier, that production of the potato spread and that it was finally appreciated as a food source on the eve of the French Revolution by a population that was starving due to food shortages. With careful planning and with the help of the King, the potato and the method of its production that Parmentier[5] had pioneered, was introduced in Anjou, Limousin, Alsace and Lorraine, and then throughout France. However, it was not until the beginning of the 19th century that the potato, cooked in oil, would finally find its place in all bourgeois households and achieve the success it enjoys today.

The epic tale of the frite

The Belgian story

Fried food on the banks of the Meuse

Just when it was taken for granted that the inventors of the frite were the French, an article[6] appeared in Belgium in the 1980s which sowed a seed of doubt and declared war between the two factions. According to the Belgian journalist Christian Souris, the very first frites were made on the banks of the Meuse, at the end of the 17th century. However, at the risk of disappointing his own people, another Belgian historian, Pierre Leclercq[7], pointed out that the economic and social context at the time made it unlikely that the population concerned would have had oil or butter in the quantities needed to deep fry. According to him, the frite was introduced by Mr Fritz, a fairground stallholder, who took it to the court at the turn of the 19th century.

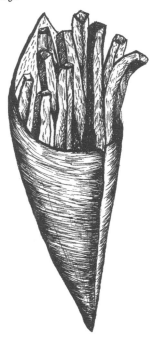

"Mr Fritz" and the popularization of fried food in Belgium

It was a certain Frederic Krieger who made fried food popular and set up the first Belgian *baraque à frites* (fried food stand) in the 1840s. After training in Paris to be a *rotisseur*, this German-born son of a fairground musician, wandered through the streets of Belgium selling his frites and promoting them at all the local fairs. He was a brilliant publicist, became known as Mr Fritz, was talked about in the local press and quickly grew his business by acquiring new establishments that he ran with his wife. And so the fried potato became extremely popular in Belgium, along with doughnuts and waffles. The term *baraque* comes from *barak* in wallonese (a Belgian dialect), and means 'a precarious construction'. These wandering street salesmen were commonplace during the Belle Epoque (the end of the 19th and beginning of the 20th centuries) and quickly spread into Northern France where potato production was rapidly developing. The potato was proving a cheap and nourishing food[8] and so, not surprisingly, the consumption of frites quickly spread amongst the middle classes. Served in a newspaper cone, the hot frites warmed people's hands. Eating them with one's fingers was an added novelty...Very quickly, everything conspired to turn the frite into the popular dish it has become in Belgium and Northern France.

Today, even if there are fewer and fewer of them, the *baraque à frites* are still part of the history of both countries. They still have a certain charm, but have swapped the newspaper cones for cardboard or plastic containers with small forks to avoid greasy fingers. In Belgium the *frituristes* have created an association, UNAFRI, to protect their profession. The country is today the biggest producer of frites in the world with 2.2 billion kilos[9] (2,200 tons) of potatoes being transformed into frites per year.

6 An article from the Belgian magazine *Pourquoi Pas,* published in 1985

7 Thanks to the Musée de la Gourmandise which gave me access to the in-depth research of Pierre Leclerc, a historian from the University of Liège

8 *La pomme de terre de la renaissance au XXIᵉs* éd Presses Universitaires François Rabelais, p.219

9 Figures taken from FEVIA (Fédération de l'Industrie Alimentaire Belge)

The epic tale of the frite

The first frites...
under the Pont Neuf

On the French side, the history of the frite is quite clear: fried potatoes were cooked for the first time under the Pont Neuf, one of the oldest bridges in Paris, during the French Revolution... This story anchors frites firmly in the history of Paris, and makes them a true symbol of France. Pont-Neuf potatoes have since become the mark of quality for genuine frites (the Parisian ones), and should be a very precise size (1 cm/ ½ in thick and 7 cm/2¾ in long).

After the French Revolution, Antoine Parmentier worked hard to make the potato popular in France, but with limited success. It remained an object of prejudice and was unappreciated by a certain sector of the population and in the end only the poorer communities used it in their cooking. It wasn't until the middle of the 19th century that it could be found at the dining tables of the bourgeoisie. As restaurants and gastronomy flourished, it grew in popularity.

Slices or sticks?

It is not clear whether the first frites, cooked under the Pont-Neuf bridge, were cut into sticks; probably not. In the first cookery book dedicated entirely to the potato, which was published after the Revolution[10], there is a recipe that is considered the very first recipe for the frite. It talks of potatoes cut into slices and deep-fried after being dipped in a doughnut batter. Potatoes cooked in oil as we know them today are not yet born. Recipes from this era mention potatoes browned in a little fat. In the literature of the early 19th century, there are references to fried fish, vegetables or meat, but not yet potatoes. It is in Antonin Carême's book[11] that a recipe for fried potatoes first appears as such. At this point 'frites' of various shapes and sizes were being sold in Paris by street vendors: *pailles* (straws), *allumettes* (matchsticks), *Pont-Neuf* or even *soufflés* (puffed); the precursor of the twice-cooked frites. The arrival of vegetable oils (notably groundnut oil from India) contributed greatly to the development of fried foods and subsequently frites took their place on the menus of Parisian brasseries, losing their status as a food for the poor and gaining that of a distinguished dish appreciated by one and all.

10 *La cuisine Républicaine,* by Mme Mérigot, 1794

11 *L'art de la cuisine Française au XIXe siècle,* 1832

Antoine Brillat **Savarin**
(1755-1826)

A true epicurean, advisor to the high court, also a chemist and doctor by training, Antoine Brillat Savarin was passionate about gastronomy, fine cuisine and top restaurants. Two months before his death he published *The Physiology of Taste, or Meditations of Transcendent Gastronomy* where he also writes about the art of cooking as a science. In this book, which was published in 1824 and was hugely successful, he discusses *les frites* ... which should be eaten with your fingers.

Auguste **Escoffier**
(1846-1935)

This man codified cooking. It is thought that he is the greatest cook of all time... He was the inventor of the peach melba, and instigator of the organized system of kitchen management. In 1902 he published his first culinary guide, still a veritable bible for today's chefs. In it you will find recipes and cooking techniques for all types of frites.

Antonin **Carême**
(1783-1833)

The first chief cook to have borne the title 'chef', this self-taught enthusiast of culinary art was nicknamed the 'Napoleon of the ovens'. Father of culinary aesthetics, he opened a new chapter in culinary publishing with his book, *The Art of Cooking in the 19th Century*, published in 1832. Cooking became more precise and above all more practical, and from now on the weight of ingredients and precise cooking times were given. It is in this book that we find the very first recipe for *pommes de terre frites* (fried potatoes), or French fries, as we also know them.

Maurice Edmond **Sailland**, dit Curnonsky
(1872-1956)

A renowned restaurant critic, he was one of the greatest defenders of French gastronomy. Founder of various Academies (of Gastronomy, of the Wines of France) he also set up the magazine *Cuisine et Vins de France*. Elected the Prince of Gastronomy, he developed the idea of simplicity in the kitchen. He is one of the great defenders of the frite as a symbol of Paris, and wrote in one of his columns in 1927: that 'Pommes de terre frites (fried potatoes) were one of the most spiritual creations of the Paris genius'.

Writers and *les frites*

Georges Duhamel, Émile Zola, Louis-Ferdinand Céline, Blaise Cendrars, Alexandre Dumas, Roland Barthes, Stendhal and even Hergé... Numerous authors have boasted about the frite throughout the 19th century, proudly elevating it to the status of a true symbol of France.

" Widely associated with steak, frites share the national limelight: both fill us with nostalgia and patriotism "

Mythologies, Roland Barthes, 1957

" And, at the bottom of this wall, in the depths of a hole, the size of a cupboard, between a scrap dealer and a fried potato vendor "

L'Assommoir, Émile Zola, 1877

" Long live Alcazar and fried potatoes "

Tintin, L'Oreille Cassée,
Hergé, 1943

" A love of frites is so Parisian "

Voyage au bout de la nuit,
Céline, 1932

The epic tale of the frite

French fries in the USA

It was Thomas Jefferson, ambassador to France at the end of the 18th century, who took the first recipe for frites home with him. As president, he served them for dinner at the White House.

But it was much later, during the First World War, that the French frite became the famous 'French fry', much cherished by the G.I.'s fighting on the Northern front. Among the many anecdotes explaining the name given to these fried sticks of potato, is the one originating from the verb 'to French' which meant, in colloquial English, 'to take off the bone, to cut up'.

A French emblem 'par excellence' in the USA, French fries were even taken hostage by restaurant owners and by American politicians when, in 2003, France stood against the war in Iraq. They were renamed 'freedom fries', a name that stuck for as long as Anglo-French relations remained strained.

And the turbulent history of frites in the New World does not end there, because the American food giants McDonald's and McCain industrialized the production of frites so successfully that these crispy little potato sticks became the very incarnation of the American way of life and its fast food, recognized worldwide ...

And elsewhere ?

• **In England**, for more than a century chips have been inseparable from the fried fish that makes up the traditional fish and chips dish. English chips are cut thicker than their American equivalent and historically were the joy of the working class who found this dish, which was served wrapped up in newspaper, wonderfully comforting. Today, the same type of absorbent paper is still used, but no longer with newsprint, in order to protect consumers from the ink.

• **In Quebec**, one of the most popular dishes since the 1950s is *poutine*, a kind of local mish-mash made from frites, melted Cheddar cheese and topped with brown sauce (made from beef stock).

• **In Italy**, they are called *patatine frite*, whilst the Portuguese have baptized them *batatas fritas*, and they eat them with a little salt and nothing else.

• As for the **Mexicans**, they like to savour their *papas a la francesa* with a little lemon juice and paprika.

• They are known as *ranskikse* in **Finland**, or as *kentang goreng* in **Malaysia,** where they are enjoyed with a little ketchup as is often the custom elsewhere.

• **In Germany**, *fritten* accompany the traditional *currywurst* (sausage curry). But you can also find *pommes rot-weiss* (red-white), which are frites served with ketchup and mayonnaise.

• And finally, in **Turkey** *patates kızartması* are savoured with lamb and the classic white sauce that comes with a *doner kebab*.

The epic tale of the frite

Avocado oil

Olive oil

Sunflower oil

Grapeseed oil

Comté cheese

Groundnut oil

Pumpkin

THE OILS

Peas

FRUIT & VEGETABLES
YOU CAN FRY

Apple

Courgette (zucchini)

Celeriac

Bananas

Sweet potato

Parsnip

The ingredients

THE POTATOES

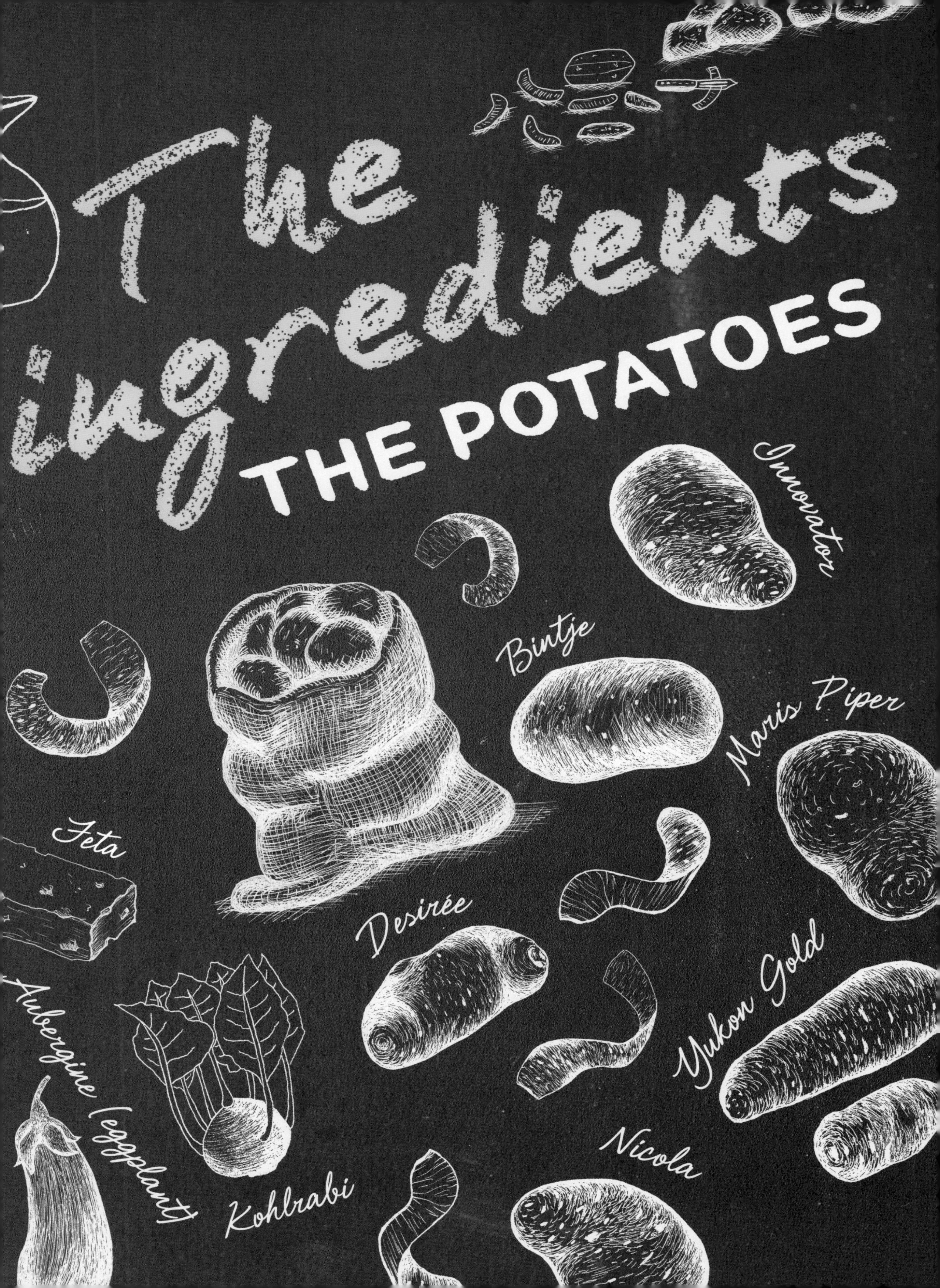

Innovator

Bintje

Maris Piper

Feta

Desirée

Yukon Gold

Aubergine (eggplant)

Kohlrabi

Nicola

THE POTATO

The potato is far more than just a comforting childhood memory. It is a major player in our gastronomic and culinary inheritance. Its nutritional qualities and its contribution to feeding people all over the world led it to be celebrated for an entire year in 2008, which was declared international Year of the Potato by the UN. In reality the potato is extremely diverse. In 1815 there were about 100 different varieties, today there are more than 4,000. Its genetic diversity never ceases to evolve thanks to the research of agricultural scientists and producers, encouraged by an ever increasing rate of global consumption. In fact, researchers have succeeded in growing potato varieties that produce almost all year round.

The numerous varieties of potato can be broken down into three main categories, which are important when it comes to cooking them: firm-fleshed, soft-fleshed and starchy potatoes. There is also a difference between potatoes that keep well (with thick skins that allow them to keep for several months after harvest and which are on sale throughout the year) and new potatoes (which are harvested before they reach maturity and therefore have a much thinner skin, the sale of which traditionally ends on July 31st each year). However, the latter are rich in water and therefore not suitable for making frites. Whilst it is difficult to tell them apart by their smell, their texture varies enormously, each containing different levels of water and sugar (glucose and fructose cause the colouring of the potato when it is fried). Those that interest us here are the all-year-round potatoes with starchy flesh, for these are the driest varieties that retain least water. The less water a potato has, the better it is for frying. It is the dryness of the potato, essentially due to the starch and sugar, which makes our frites crispy. The starch content depends on the size (or grade) of the potato: the larger the size, the more starch the potato will have. A high level of starch limits the absorption of oil during cooking. Not an insignificant detail. A potato of between 5.5–6.5 cm (2–2½ in) long is a good size for a starchy-fleshed potato that is ideal for cutting nice, long frites. Firm-fleshed potatoes are ideal for oven cooking, which requires far less oil.

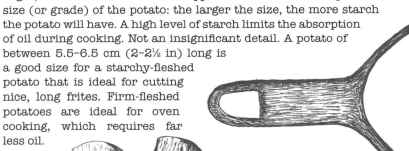

The ingredients

● Choose **a variety** that is harvested when completely mature and kept through the winter.

● Choose a **starchy variety**, with flesh that loosens enough on cooking to create a frite which is soft on the inside and crispy on the outside. Avoid any variety with firm flesh or soft flesh, both of which remain firm on cooking.

● **A good size**, with a slightly oblong or elongated shape and unbroken skin.

● A good **dry potato**, which will crisp up well when cooked. But not too 'starchy' either or it risks resulting in frites that are too dry.

How to keep **POTATOES** :

Our eating habits have evolved: these days we expect nice, clean potatoes and this is why those sold in our supermarkets are, more often than not, sold ready washed. But this makes them porous and more fragile to keep.

● Don't keep your potatoes for too long. The more starchy potatoes tend to accumulate slow sugars as they are kept. These sugars cause them to brown too quickly when you fry them and prevent them cooking properly.

● To protect them, keep potatoes out of the light and in a cool room, between 5°C and 8°C (41°F and 46.4°F), such as a cellar, a shed (outhouse) or a larder (pantry).

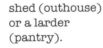

The ingredients

The different POTATO varieties :

INNOVATOR (RUSSET)

● **Shape :** long, oval shaped

● **Flesh :** pale yellow flesh and russet skin

MARIS PIPER (WHITE)

● **Shape :** oval shaped

● **Flesh :** cream flesh and skin

DESIRÉE (RED)

● **Shape :** oval shaped

● **Flesh :** light yellow flesh

BINTJE, QUEEN OF ALL POTATOES

This is the most popular potato in France and Belgium (the queen of the famous Belgian *baraque à frites*). More than 100 years old, it originates from the Netherlands and remains the frite chef's best friend in the kitchen, the most versatile potato of all. Its low water content and large size makes it the best choice when it comes to frites. A good substitute is Yukon Gold, if you can't find Bintje in the supermarket.

● **Shape :** oblong

● **Flesh :** yellow flesh and skin

YUKON GOLD (GOLD)

- **Shape :** large, round or oval shaped
- **Flesh :** creamy yellow flesh and skin

NiCOLA (SALAD)

(firm flesh, ideal for oven cooking)

- **Shape :** oblong
- **Flesh :** yellow flesh and skin

FRUITS & VEGETABLES
YOU CAN FRY

You can make frites from more than just potatoes. Numerous other vegetables, as well as certain fruits, are delicious fried. The important thing for other vegetables is that they should be tubers, that is to say root vegetables or those that grow underground (like our dear potato) as this will ensure the low moisture content that is so important for a successful frite. Carrots, parsnips and other ancient vegetables that are easily found today are therefore a delight served up fried. Other vegetables and fruits, with a higher moisture content, can still be fried, as long as they are coated in breadcrumbs first, in a similar way to cheese. Oven cooking is also a good way to 'fry' lots of foods by simply coating them in oil. This cooking method is a great way to make slightly lighter frites as they are not fully immersed in oil.

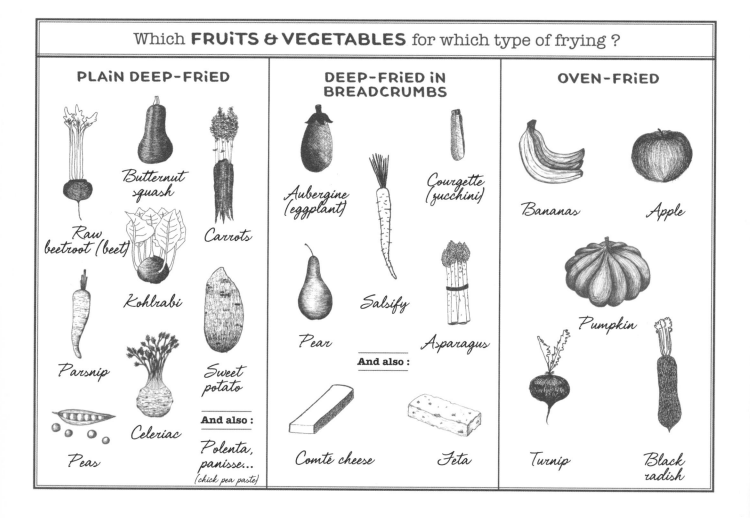

Which FRUITS & VEGETABLES for which type of frying ?

PLAIN DEEP-FRIED

Butternut squash

Raw beetroot (beet)

Carrots

Kohlrabi

Parsnip

Sweet potato

And also :

Celeriac

Peas

Polenta, panisse...
(chick pea paste)

DEEP-FRIED IN BREADCRUMBS

Aubergine (eggplant)

Courgette (zucchini)

Salsify

Pear

Asparagus

And also :

Comté cheese

Feta

OVEN-FRIED

Bananas

Apple

Pumpkin

Turnip

Black radish

Fruit & veg to fry

Kohlrabi
Butternut squash
Sweet potato
Parsnip
Celeriac
Beetroot (beet)
Carrots...

OILS

When a food is deep-fried in oil, the water on its surface evaporates, creating a nice golden crust. The oil is heated beyond its boiling point, so it is very important to choose your oil carefully.

Sunflower oil

Using an electric fryer, which comes with a built-in thermostat, or a traditional deep fryer and a culinary thermometer, will allow you to make delicious frites without exceeding recommended temperatures.

A good oil for frying should be rich in saturated fatty acids: this makes it more stable for cooking and means it will last longer (groundnut oil, for example). But some of the oils, known as 'mono-saturated' (which are better for our arteries), can also be used for frying (olive oil, for example, which also has less odour).

It is also better to choose a reasonably priced oil and to avoid, where possible, cold-pressed and extra virgin oils, which are more fragile and lose their nutritional values when heated to very high temperatures.

The best way to find out whether an oil is good for frying is to determine its smoking point, in other words, the temperature at which the oil begins to smoke (see pages 28–29).

Groundnut oil

It follows then, that an oil that can withstand high temperatures, 160 °C to 180 °C (320°F to 356°F), is essential for deep-frying. In fact, most oils have a smoking point of around 200°C (392°F), which means that as long as you don't heat your oil beyond 180°C (356°F) – the ideal temperature for good frites – you won't be taking any risks or creating a fire hazard.

Olive oil

Many purists still swear by using animal fat (which does give an incomparable taste to your frites … in Belgium beef suet or horse fat are still used), but nutritionists advise against using these fats, even though they make delicious frites. Furthermore, they are hard to find these days. In the south-west of France, goose fat is sometimes used – fortunately this is not considered harmful as long as you don't overdo it and keep the temperature below 190°C (374°F) when cooking.

It is essential to change your cooking oil regularly. Used oil is not only toxic but also becomes more viscous than fresh oil: which means more of it clings to the food, making it greasier and less easily digested. For oven-cooking, the oil simply coats the food and is not in direct contact with the heat source, therefore it withstands higher temperatures better. It is still advisable, however, to use an appropriate oil, such as olive oil, which is ideal for oven-cooked frites.

Avocado oil

Grapeseed oil

Which type of OIL for which type of frying ?

SUNFLOWER OiL :

🌑 With a neutral taste, this withstands high temperatures well. Today you can find special varieties for deep-frying, which are rich in oleic acid, making them more stable, or with essence of coriander (cilantro), which is odourless.

🌑 Change after 2 or 3 uses.

🌑 **Smoking point :** 180°C (356°F)

OLiVE OiL :

🌑 This has a fairly pronounced taste, and is not often used for frying, but it is worth trying. It's an oil that is highly recommended for its nutritional value and perfect for making oven-baked frites.

🌑 Change after 2 or 3 uses.

🌑 **Smoking point :** 190°C (374°F)

GROUNDNUT OiL :

🌑 This has a neutral taste and stands up well to high temperatures. However, it is high in saturated fats and should be used in moderation. It can also trigger allergic reactions and should be avoided by those with nut allergies.

🌑 Change after 5 or 6 uses maximum.

🌑 **Smoking point :** 230°C (446°F)

GRAPESEED OiL :

🌑 This has a neutral taste and stands up well to very high temperatures. But it is expensive and therefore rarely used on its own: it is frequently mixed with sunflower oil, which gives it a good cooking consistency.

🌑 When mixed with sunflower oil it should be changed after 5 or 6 uses.

🌑 **Smoking point :** 210°C (410°F)

AVOCADO OiL :

🌑 Its delicate taste is incomparable. This is one of the most stable cold-pressed vegetable oils at high temperature. But it is not easy to find and is therefore quite expensive.

🌑 Change after 2 or 3 uses.

🌑 **Smoking point :** 225°C (437°F)

pommes allumettes

Pont-Neuf potatoes

traditional fryer

chopping board

kitchen paper

Cooking

electric fryer

potato cutter

scoop for frites

semi-professional fryer

frying basket

skinny frites

PEELING

cooking thermometer

colander for frites

Technical guide

tea towel

kitchen knife

standard knife

potato peeler

metal bowl

vegetable brush

colander

vegetable peeler

scrubbing glove

CLEANING

Proper cleaning is an important step in making good frites. It is done in several phases, starting with an initial rinse before the potatoes are peeled. The potatoes you buy in the supermarket may well have been pre-washed. As the potatoes used for frites tend to have thicker skins and are often covered in earth, this initial rinse before peeling is important, especially if you plan to cook them in their skins. If you buy your potatoes directly from the producer, they are less likely to be pre-washed. If this is the case, wash them carefully yourself using a special vegetable brush. Once peeled, the potatoes need to be carefully rinsed again to rid them of their starch and prevent them sticking to one another. Leave them to soak for 30 minutes in cold water. Then, once they have been cut up, they will need several rinses to remove the rest of the starch. Finally, it is absolutely essential to dry them carefully so that they are totally dry when dropped into the hot oil. Any moisture in the vegetables will significantly lower the temperature of the oil as they cook, which prevents them from frying properly. If the oil is not hot enough, it will be absorbed by the vegetable, instead of forming a nice crisp exterior.

EQUIPMENT

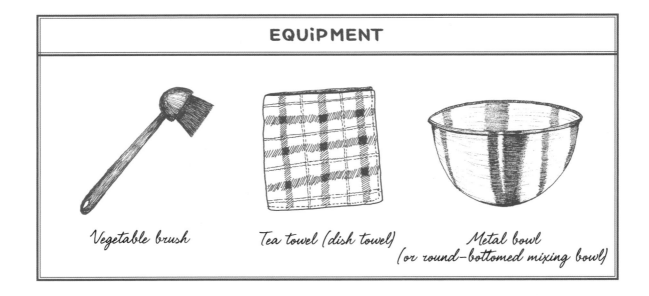

Vegetable brush

Tea towel (dish towel)

Metal bowl
(or round-bottomed mixing bowl)

Technical guide

Steps for
CLEANiNG :

STEP 1
Rinse + scrub (if necessary) before peeling.

STEP 2
1st soak in cold water for 30 minutes (potatoes are still whole).

STEP 3
2nd soak in cold water (potatoes are cut up), then rinse immediately.

STEP 4
3rd and 4th rinse in cold water until the water runs clear.

STEP 5
Dry the potatoes carefully with a clean, dry cloth. Each potato stick must be completely dry.

Colander

Metal bowl (or round-bottomed mixing bowl)

Vegetable brush

PEELING

Traditionally, frites are cooked without their skins. And it is indeed healthier to eat potatoes without their skins as the first 3 mm (⅛ in) are full of harmful sugars (glycoalkaloids). Our great grandmothers would have used a simple kitchen knife for peeling potatoes, but the invention of the potato peeler in the 1930s made things a lot easier. "Econome", meaning economic, is the French word for potato peeler and a registered trademark for the straight peeler widely used today. This design has been greatly copied and modernized to create all kinds of vegetable peelers, which allow anyone to dispense with the chore of peeling potatoes quickly and efficiently. There are even models that help you peel even more easily thanks to a tiny motor hidden in the handle. Another very practical little accessory is the scrubbing glove, made of sticky silicone. It allows you to remove fine vegetable skin by simply rubbing. Some professionals have mchines that can peel several kilos (pounds) of potatoes at a time. However, peeling by hand is still preferred in good restaurants as it is the only way to remove all the eyes – tiny seed tubers – which are often found deep inside the potato and thus inaccessible to a machine.

The **"ECONOME"** potato peeling knife, a French invention

An advertising poster in the 1960s boasted "30% of your time and your potatoes saved". The stainless steel potato peeling knife, which allows you to peel off fine strips of skin and therefore keep more of the flesh, was invented by the Frenchman Victor Pouzet in Thiers (birthplace of the cutlery industry in France). It is still produced by the brand Thieras, but its design has been modernized due to the availability of different materials and more diverse colours for the handle.

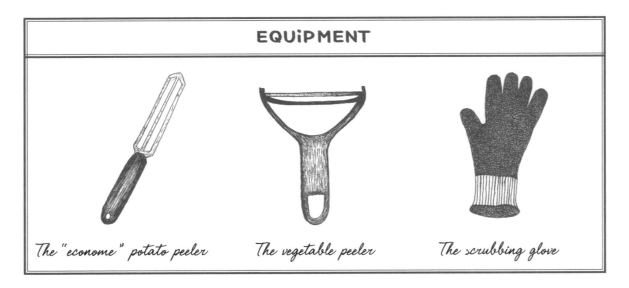

EQUIPMENT

The "econome" potato peeler   The vegetable peeler   The scrubbing glove

Technical guide

CUTTiNG

The next important stage in the preparation of frites is the way they are cut. We have already seen that there are several possible types of frite, and so it is important to cut them with care to get the exact size and shape that you want. Using a traditional kitchen knife will give you more irregular shaped frites, which some argue gives them a special taste. Because the size varies, so does the cooking time, and so smaller frites will be cooked more than the bigger ones. This variation in size looks appealing and makes the dish of frites look more authentic. However, the invention of the potato cutter some 100 years ago, with its interchangeable cutters, allows you to cut perfect frites in one quick action. Thanks to its manual lever, this accessory can transform a potato into evenly-cut sticks in less than 5 seconds. Some food processors have an additional attachment for chopping vegetables into julienne strips, which are excellent for making very fine frites, or 'pommes pailles' as they are known in France.

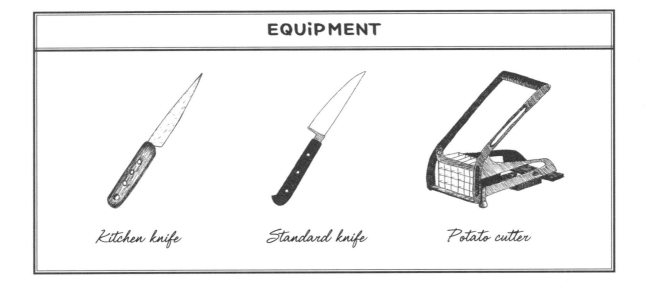

EQUiPMENT

Kitchen knife   Standard knife   Potato cutter

Technical guide

STEP 1

Square off the potato :
Cut away the rounded edges on each side to make the potato a rectangular shape. This will allow you to have more evenly cut frites.

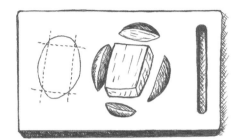

STEP 2

Cut the slices : place the potato on a chopping board and, using a standard knife, cut the potato into slices lengthways. The thickness of the slices will depend on whether you are making thick cut frites (Pont-Neuf potatoes) or thinner cut frites (*pommes pailles* or *allumettes*).

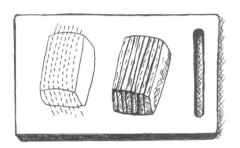

STEP 3

Place the slices one on top of the other and cut sticks by sliding the knife from the top to the bottom of each slice.

Which **KNiFE** for cutting ?

There are numerous knives of all shapes and sizes, for various different tasks in the kitchen. Here are the best ones to use for cutting potatoes or other vegetables into sticks for frying :

• **The chef's knife or kitchen knife** : has a wide blade, is about 20 cm (8 in) long, and allows you to cut into the thick, firm flesh of a potato or other root vegetable (such as a sweet potato) with ease.

• **The standard knife** : has a narrower and shorter blade. It usually measures about 9 cm or 10 cm (3½ in or 4 in) and is better suited for cutting smaller potatoes.

STANDARD MEASUREMENTS for frites

(according to Auguste Escoffier)

POMMES PAiLLES :
Potatoes cut into long, thin strips like straws

POMMES ALLUMETTES :
5 mm (¼ in) sticks

PONT-NEUF POTATOES:
1 cm (½ in) sticks

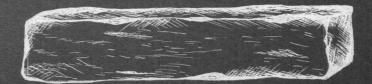

COOKiNG

And now the final step: frying. This ancient cooking method can be traced back to the Egyptians. A saucepan of oil is heated to a high temperature, which will seal the potato and evaporate all its moisture. This dehydrating action causes an outside crust to form, allowing the inside to stay nice and soft. Unlike water, for which the boiling point is no more than 100°C (212°F), oil can reach temperatures two or three times higher. But, as explained previously, the ideal temperature is no higher than 180°C (356°F) to avoid deterioration of the potatoes. Our grandmothers would have used a basic saucepan and basket to make frites. The traditionalists among us may still use this method, using a cooking thermometer to monitor the temperature along with a cast-iron pan and basket for the frites. However, in the 1960s a well-known French brand gave a whole new life to fried food with the invention of the electric fryer. Equipped with a thermostat, a lid and an anti-odour filter, the electric fryer allows you to make frites quickly and simply, without smells (more or less) and, above all, safely. Various models have since evolved, with a large range of high tech and sleek designs on the market that rival professional machines.

THE KEY STAGES for cooking frites

Traditionally, frites are always cooked twice. The only down side of this is that the potato absorbs twice the amount of oil. If you want to lighten your frites, you can cook them just once at 170°C (338°F).

1st cooking : lower the frites into the oil, previously heated to 140°C or 150°C (284°F or 302°F), for 5 to 7 minutes (the exact timing will depend on the thickness of your frites). Remove and allow to cool for 30 minutes.

2nd cooking : lower the frites back into the oil, which has now been heated to 170°C or 180°C (338°F or 356°F). Fry for 5 to 7 minutes depending on their thickness.

How to choose your FRYER

FILTERS :

There are various types of filter: permanent ones that can be put through the dishwasher, and disposable ones. Bear in mind, however, that whatever the filter, some cooking smells are inevitable in the room you are cooking in. The best solution is either to use the fryer in a separate room with a window or, ideally, outside.

CAPACITY :

A traditional fryer can cook between 500 g (1 lb) and 1 kg (2.2 lb) of fresh frites, depending on the model. Some family-size machines can cope with up to 2 kg (4.4 lb) of frites in one go. You will need between 2 and 3 litres (8½ cups and 12¼ cups) of oil to fill the pan.

SAFETY :

The fryer must be set up on a flat, stable surface; on no account should it be moved during use. Wait for 2 to 3 hours after cooking for the oil to completely cool, should you need to move it.

ODOURLESS, FAT-FREE FRYERS :

It was the same well-known French brand that came up with another new idea for frying when it invented the first odourless, fat-free fryer in 2006. It functions by cooking with a system of hot air and infra-red radiation and the frites only need 1 or 2 tablespoons of oil. This means the potatoes are not swimming in hot fat: the resulting frites contain less than 3% fat and there are no lingering frying smells.

EQUIPMENT

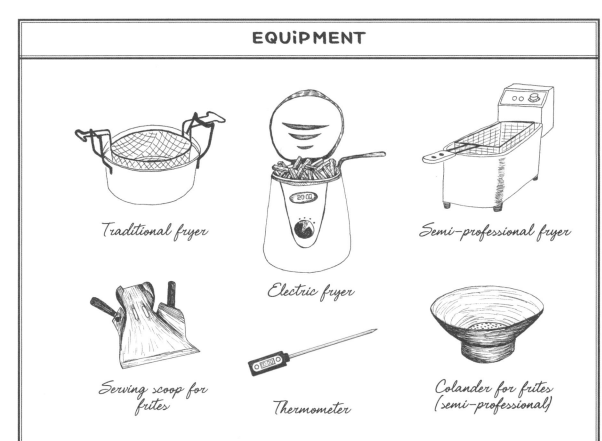

Traditional fryer

Electric fryer

Semi-professional fryer

Serving scoop for frites

Thermometer

Colander for frites (semi-professional)

Other cooking METHODS

We can thank the McCain Company who, having invented frozen frites, went on to invent oven frites. Oven-cooking was no longer just an alternative to deep-frying but became a genuine method of cooking frites, preferred by many. Like the fat-free fryer, it provided a low-fat method of cooking potatoes and other vegetables without immersing them in oil. Fresh frites simply need to be brushed with oil before popping them in the oven. Frozen frites are already oiled, which saves a lot of time. Certain vegetables that make delicious frites are even better cooked delicately in the oven than they are in the fryer. You simply spread the frites out across an oven dish and pop them into the oven for the time indicated, remembering to turn them halfway through cooking. Special baskets are also available that attach to a rotisserie arm and rotate during cooking, so that the frites are constantly turned.

Tradition frites

FRENCH PONT-NEUF

BELGIA

AMERICAN FRENCH

Englis

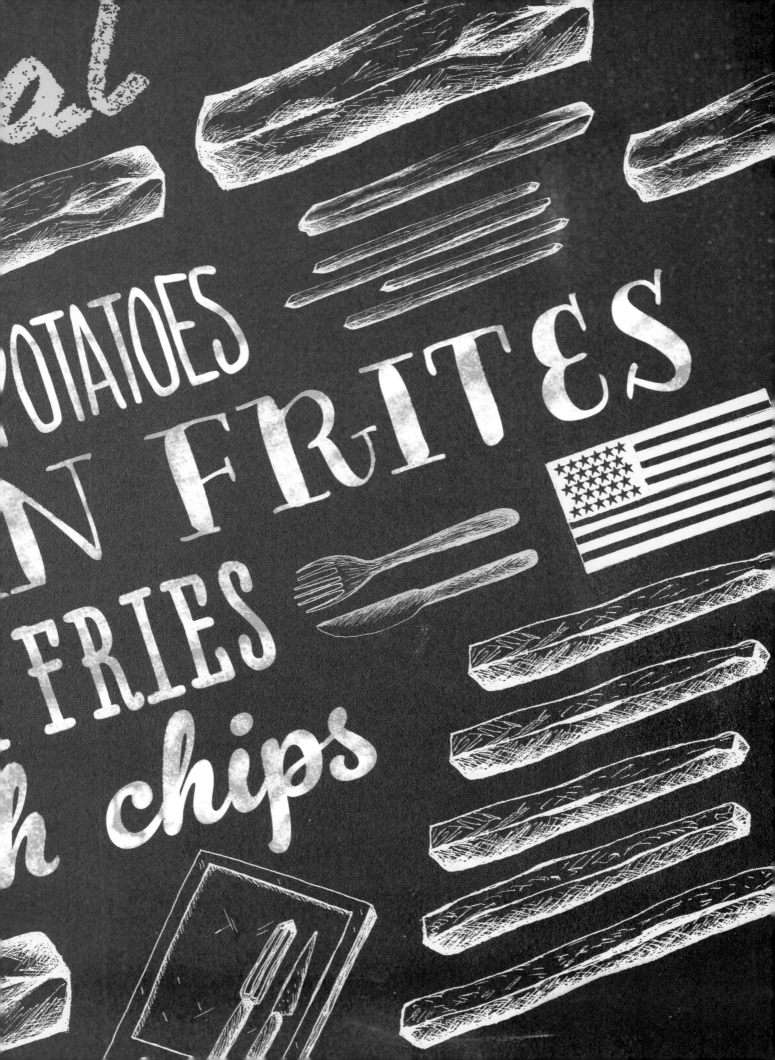

FRENCH PONT-NEUF POTATOES

4 / 15 / 10 / 30 RESTING

1 KG (2.2 LB) BINTJE, YUKON GOLD OR SIMILAR POTATOES
2 LITRES (8¼ CUPS) OF COOKING OIL
½ TSP OF TABLE SALT
½ TSP OF SEA SALT CRYSTALS

● **Peel** and wash the potatoes. Use a knife to cut them into 1-cm (½-in) thick sticks. Or if you have one, use a potato cutter.

● **Rinse** the potatoes several times to get rid of the starch (the last rinsing water should run clear) and then dry them carefully with a clean, dry cloth.

● **Pour** the oil into the deep fryer and heat to 150°C (302°F). Place the dried potato pieces in the basket. Avoid putting too many in at a time: 1 kg (2.2 lb) of potatoes should be cooked in two batches.

● **Lower** the basket into the fryer and cook for 7 minutes.

● **Lift out the basket** and shake well to toss the potatoes and drain them. Then leave to cool for about 30 minutes.

● **Reheat the oil** to 180°C (356°F) and cook again for no longer than 3 minutes.

● **Remove the fried potatoes,** shaking well to drain them. Then tip them into a large bowl lined with kitchen paper. Remove the paper and salt generously with the table salt. Leave to cool briefly and then serve while still hot, adding the sea salt at the last moment.

THESE GO WELL WITH :
    FRITE SAUCE
    HOMEMADE KETCHUP
    BÉARNAISE SAUCE
    FRESH HERB SAUCE

SECRETS OF A GOOD STEAK-FRITES

The traditional French steak is a 1.5-cm (⅝-in) thick rump (sirloin) steak cooked on a ridged griddle pan (or a barbeque grill) giving it an attractive criss-cross pattern on each side. Brush a little oil on each side of the steak using a pastry brush. Add salt and pepper and cook on a hot ridged griddle pan for about 2 minutes on each side. To make the criss-cross effect, place the steak perpendicular to the griddle for 1 minute and then horizontally for another minute. To turn the steak, spear it through the fat on the side, rather than through the meat, in order to avoid losing any meat juices.

Traditional frites

Bearnaise sauce

BELGIAN FRITES

1 KG (2.2 LB) BiNTJE, YUKON GOLD OR SiMiLAR POTATOES

**2 LiTRES (8¼ CUPS) OF COOKiNG OiL
(OR BEEF SUET FOR THE PURiSTS)**

½ TSP OF TABLE SALT

½ TSP OF SEA SALT CRYSTALS

● **Peel** and wash the potatoes.

● **Cut** them into medium-sized sticks with a kitchen knife or use a potato cutter.

● **Wash** them thoroughly by leaving them to soak in cold water for 30 minutes. Repeat this process several times to remove all the starch (the water used for the last soak should remain clear) and then dry them carefully with a clean, dry cloth.

● **Heat** the fryer to 140 °C (284 °F). Place the dried potato pieces into the basket.

● **Lower** the basket into the fryer and cook for 7 minutes. Lift out the basket, shake well to toss and drain the frites and leave to cool for about 30 minutes.

● **Reheat** the oil to 170 °C (338 °F) and cook a second time for no longer than 3 minutes. Your frites should be perfectly crisp.

● **Remove** the frites, shaking well to drain them. Then tip them into a large bowl lined with kitchen paper.

● **Salt** generously with table salt. Add a sprinkle of sea salt just before serving.

THESE GO WELL WiTH :
    FRiTE SAUCE
    HOMEMADE KETCHUP
    ONiON SAUCE
    TANGY TOMATO SAUCE

> **AUTHENTiC "MOULES-FRiTES"**
>
> The traditional Belgian dish of mussels with frites is a must. The mussels are simple to prepare: finely chop 2 onions and 3 good sticks of celery. Fry lightly in a little butter. Season with salt and pepper, then add 11 mussels, previously washed and sorted. Cover and leave to cook until all have opened. Throw away any that remain closed, adjust the seasoning and enjoy.

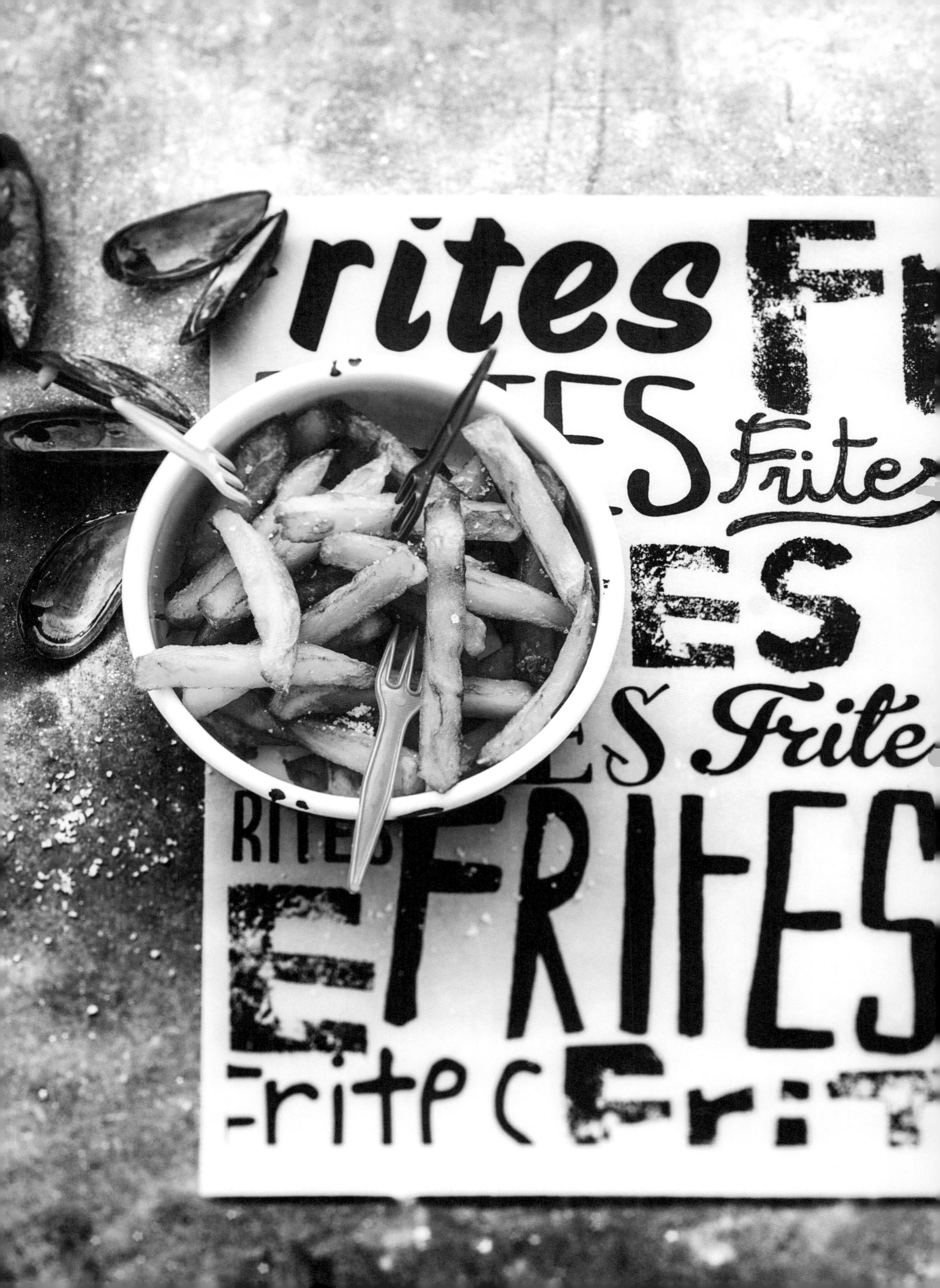
rites
Frite
Frite
RITES
FRITES

ENGLISH CHIPS

4   15   5   8   30 RESTING

1 KG (2.2 LB) BINTJE, YUKON GOLD OR SIMILAR POTATOES

2 LITRES (8½ CUPS) OF COOKING OIL

½ TSP OF TABLE SALT

½ TSP OF SEA SALT CRYSTALS

● **Peel** and wash the potatoes. Rinse several times to remove the starch, the last water should run clear.

● **Cut** the potatoes into neat sticks of equal size. Use a potato cutter if you have one.

● **Blanch** them in a large saucepan of boiling water. Remove with a draining spoon and rinse immediately with cold water to stop further cooking.

● **Drain** and dry well with a clean, dry cloth.

● **Heat** the fryer to 150°C (302°F) and tip the pre-cooked potatoes into the basket. Be careful not to put too many in at a time.

● **Lower** the basket into the fryer and cook for 5 minutes. As the potato sticks have been blanched first, they will cook very quickly.

● **Lift** out the basket, shake well in order to toss and drain the chips, and leave to cool for about 30 minutes.

● **Reheat** the oil to 180°C (356°F) and put the chips back in to cook for no longer than 3 minutes.

● **Remove** the chips, shake again to drain them well and tip into a large bowl lined with kitchen paper. Use more kitchen paper to dab them carefully if you want to remove more oil. Tip onto a serving dish and salt generously with table salt.

● **Serve** immediately while piping hot and add a sprinkle of sea salt at the last minute.

THESE GO WELL WITH :
FRITE SAUCE
HOMEMADE KETCHUP
CURRY SAUCE
TARTAR SAUCE

THE REAL RECIPE FOR FISH & CHIPS

Delicious fried and served with 'chips', the famous 'fish & chips' is made using fillets of white fish (cod or haddock) dipped in batter made with beer. The batter puffs up as it cooks, making a perfect coating around the fish. For the batter: mix 400 g (3¼ cups) of flour with salt and pepper in a bowl. Add 250 ml (1 cup) of good quality beer and 250 ml (1 cup) of carbonated water. Stir well and leave aside for half an hour. Dip the fish pieces into the flour and then the batter, just before frying them. Serve with tartar sauce and accompany the 'chips' with malt vinegar.

Traditional frites

Malt vinegar

AMERICAN FRENCH FRIES

1 KG (2.2 LB) OF RUSSET POTATOES, SUCH AS iNNOVATOR

2 LiTRES (8¼ CUPS) OF COOKiNG OiL

½ TSP OF TABLE SALT

½ TSP OF SEA SALT CRYSTALS

● **Peel** the potatoes and cut them into fine sticks. If using a potato cutter, choose the finest setting.

● **Place** the fries in a bowl of cold water and soak for 30 minutes. Rinse several times. Dry carefully with a clean, dry cloth. Heat the fryer to 150°C (302°F). Place the potatoes in the basket, taking care not to overfill it.

● **Lower** the basket and leave to fry for 7 minutes. Lift out the basket, shake the fries well to air them and leave to cool for 30 minutes.

● **Reheat** the oil to 180°C (356°F) and cook again for no longer than 3 minutes.

● **Remove** the fries, drain them and tip into a large bowl lined with kitchen paper. Remove the paper and salt generously with table salt.

● **Serve** immediately with sea salt sprinkled over.

THESE GO WELL WiTH :
   FRiTE SAUCE
   HOMEMADE KETCHUP
   TANGY TOMATO SAUCE
   TARTAR SAUCE

THE AMERiCAN HAMBURGER RECiPE

Inseparable from its French fries, the American hamburger is delicious prepared on the spot with freshly minced (ground) beef. Mix the minced (ground) beef with a little Worcestershire sauce, some finely chopped onions and ground cumin. With your hands, pat the meat into an oval burger shape. Cook directly on a grill or in a frying pan (skillet) – no need for oil. Add a slice of Cheddar at the last minute and let it melt over the burger. Serve up in a toasted hamburger bun spread with a little ketchup and mayonnaise. Add a piece of lettuce, two slices of tomato, a pickled gherkin and grilled (broiled) bacon ... Serve piping hot.

Tangy tomato sauce

U.S. ARMY

Green pea frites

aubergine (eggp

FETA FRIT

CARAMELIZED HO

POLENTA FRITES

ASHED POTATO FRIT

POMMES PA

Extra

ASPARAGUS FRITES

ant) frites

ES

NEY FRITES

Trendy
frites

ILES – SKINNY F

rispy frites Courgette (zucchini)
parmesan
and poppy seed
frites

CARROT FRITES

POMMES PAILLES OR SKINNY FRITES

1 KG (2.2 LB) OF BiNTJE, YUKON GOLD OR SiMiLAR POTATOES

2 LiTRES (8¼ CUPS) OF COOKiNG OiL

TABLE SALT

SEA SALT CRYSTALS

- **Peel** and wash the potatoes.

- **Use a mandolin** to cut them into thin slices, then cut each slice into fine sticks 1.5 mm to 2 mm (1/16 in to 1/8 in) wide. Soak in cold water for 30 minutes and then rinse several times. Dry carefully with a clean, dry cloth.

- **Heat the fryer** to 160°C (320°F).

- **Put** the frites in the basket and cook for 5 minutes.

- **Spread** the frites onto kitchen paper then sprinkle with table salt.

- **Tip into a serving dish,** add a sprinkle of sea salt and eat straightaway.

THESE GO WELL WiTH :
   FRiTE SAUCE
   HOMEMADE KETCHUP
   AiOLi

> **TOP TiP...**
>
> You can make 'pommes cheveux' ('hair' or 'shoestring' frites) in the same way. Just cut them even finer (1 mm/1/32 in). A good trick is to use a julienne slicer but, if you do, be warned that the sticks tend to curl rather than remain straight.

Homemade ketchup

EXTRA CRISPY
FRITES

4 15 30 8

1 KG (2.2 LB) OF DESIREE (RED) POTATOES

2 EGGS

2 TBSP OF FLOUR

3 TBSP OF BREADCRUMBS

2 TBSP OF PARMESAN, GRATED

2 LITRES (8¼ CUPS) OF COOKING OIL

1 TSP OF TABLE SALT

½ TSP OF SEA SALT CRYSTALS

⬤ **Peel** the potatoes then wash them quickly under cold water. Use a knife to cut them into medium-sized sticks, taking care to keep them roughly the same size. A manual potato cutter is ideal as it makes identically sized sticks.

⬤ **Soak** the sticks in cold water for 30 minutes. Rinse several times to get rid of the starch and then dry them carefully with a clean, dry cloth.

⬤ **Heat** the fryer to 180°C (356°F).

⬤ **Beat the eggs** in a large bowl. Put the flour into a second bowl and the bread-crumbs, Parmesan and salt mixed together in a third.

⬤ **Coat** each frite by dipping it first in the flour, next in the eggs and, finally, in the breadcrumb mixture. Then place it carefully in the frying basket.

⬤ **Lower the basket** and fry for 8 minutes. Lift out the basket, shake gently to drain the frites and place them in a large bowl lined with kitchen paper. Remove the paper.

⬤ **Salt** the frites lightly with sea salt and eat piping hot.

THESE GO WELL WITH :
    FRITE SAUCE
    HOMEMADE KETCHUP
    BÉARNAISE SAUCE
    BLUE CHEESE SAUCE

> **TOP TIP...**
>
> You can vary the taste of these frites by adding different flavours to the batter. The only constraint: use dry ingredients (no fresh herbs). You could try adding ¼ tsp of dried garlic, shallots or even dried basil.

Extra *crispy frites*

4

10

20

1 KG (2.2 LB) OF NICOLA
POTATOES

2 TSP OF PARMESAN,
GRATED

1 TSP OF DRIED THYME

3 TBSP OF OLIVE OIL

SEA SALT CRYSTALS

FRESHLY GROUND BLACK
PEPPER

THYME AND
PARMESAN FRITES

🔸 **Preheat** the oven to 180 °C (350°F /gas 4).

🔸 **Peel** the potatoes and soak them in cold water. Rinse thoroughly and, using a knife, cut thick, wide slices that you can then cut into fairly chunky sticks (about 12 mm/½ in wide).

🔸 **Rinse the sticks** again, dry carefully with a clean, dry cloth and put them in a large bowl. Pour over the olive oil and stir well to make sure they are all coated.

🔸 **Sprinkle** with the Parmesan and the thyme then put the oiled frites carefully into a freezer bag. Close it tightly and shake thoroughly so that the cheese and herbs stick to the frites. Open the bag to add salt and pepper. Close and shake thoroughly again.

🔸 **Spread** out on a baking sheet covered with greaseproof (parchment) paper.

🔸 **Cook in the preheated oven** for 20 minutes.

🔸 **Check the seasoning** at the end of the cooking time and enjoy immediately.

THESE GO WELL WITH :
    FRITE SAUCE
    ONION SAUCE

4

10

5

1H
RESTING

200 G (1¼ CUPS) OF GREEN
PEAS (CANNED OR FROZEN)

A DASH OF OLIVE OIL

200 G (2 CUPS) OF FLOUR

120 ML (½ CUP) OF WATER

½ TSP GROUND CUMIN

2 LITRES (8½ CUPS) OF
COOKING OIL

SEA SALT CRYSTALS

FRESHLY GROUND
BLACK PEPPER

GREEN PEA FRITES

🔸 **Drain** the peas if you are using canned ones or blanch quickly in boiling water if using frozen ones.

🔸 **Make a thick purée** with the cooked peas, adding just a dash of olive oil. Add the flour, water, cumin, salt and pepper and mix well.

🔸 **Spread the pea purée** out on a baking sheet, to make an even layer about 2 cm (¾ in) thick, and leave to cool. Put in the fridge for 1 hour.

🔸 **Heat the fryer** to 170°C (338°F). Cut long strips out of the chilled pea purée and cut again to make 10 cm (4 in) long frites. Place these in the frying basket.

🔸 **Fry** for 5 minutes and then tip into a large bowl lined with kitchen paper. Remove the paper.

🔸 **Check the seasoning** and enjoy whilst piping hot.

THESE GO WELL WITH :
    HOMEMADE KETCHUP
    TARTAR SAUCE
    BARBECUE SAUCE

MASHED POTATO
FRITES

4

15

5

1H
RESTING

1 KG (2.2 LB) OF BINTJE, YUKON GOLD OR SIMILAR POTATOES

2 TBSP OF FLOUR

2 EGGS

3 TBSP OF DRIED BREADCRUMBS

2 LITRES (8¼ CUPS) OF COOKING OIL

TABLE SALT

SEA SALT CRYSTALS

● **Peel** the potatoes and wash them thoroughly in cold water. Cut into quarters and drop into boiling water. Check that they are cooked by piercing with the point of a sharp knife.

● **Mash the potatoes** into a smooth, stiff purée. To keep it dry, don't use milk or butter. Add salt and mix well.

● **Spread** this purée out on a baking sheet to form an even 2-cm (¾-in) thick layer and leave to cool. Then put it in the fridge for 1 hour.

● **Heat** the fryer to 180°C (356°F).

● **Cut out** your frites from the chilled purée. Put the flour in one bowl, beat the eggs in a second bowl and put the breadcrumbs in a third. Add a little salt to each bowl. Take the mashed potato frites carefully one by one using your fingers (or tongs) and dip them in the flour, then the eggs and finally the breadcrumbs.

● **Put them in the fryer basket,** spacing them out carefully so they don't touch. Lower the basket into the fryer and cook for no more than 5 minutes. Lift out the basket, shake to drain the frites and lay them on a plate covered with kitchen paper, sprinkle with table salt. Remove the paper.

● **Salt** lightly with the sea salt and eat while piping hot.

THESE GO WELL WITH :
    FRITE SAUCE
    HOMEMADE KETCHUP
    BÉARNAISE SAUCE
    TANGY TOMATO SAUCE
    BARBECUE SAUCE

TOP TIP...

For a creamier texture you can add a béchamel sauce to your purée and even flavour it with Parmesan, Roquefort, crushed olives or tomato sauce. Always ensure that the mixture is quite dry, so that you can make frites that will hold together during cooking.

Béarnaise sauce

CARAMELIZED HONEY
FRITES

1 KG (2.2 LB) OF NiCOLA (SALAD) POTATOES

1 TBSP OF HONEY

3 TBSP OF OLiVE OiL

SEA SALT CRYSTALS

FRESHLY GROUND BLACK PEPPER

● **Preheat** the oven to 180°C (350°F/gas 4).

● **Peel** the potatoes and soak them for one minute in cold water. Rinse them thoroughly, cut into large slices and then trim into medium-sized sticks (about 1 cm/½ in). Wash and dry carefully with a clean, dry cloth, then tip into a large bowl.

● **Pour over** the olive oil and mix well so that the frites are well covered with oil. Season generously with salt and pepper, add the honey and mix again.

● **Put** the frites on a baking sheet lined with greaseproof (parchment) paper, spacing them out well.

● **Bake in the preheated oven,** on a high shelf, for 10 minutes. Keep an eye on them whilst cooking to make sure the honey doesn't burn. As soon as they start to caramelize, remove from the oven.

● **Season** if necessary and serve straightaway.

THESE GO WELL WiTH :
  FRiTE SAUCE
  ONiON SAUCE
  SOY SAUCE

TOP TiP...

This recipe is good for chunky American wedges in their skins. Wash and scrub the potatoes and cut them into quarters without peeling them. Coat them with olive oil, honey and paprika and then pop them in the oven for 15 minutes at 180°C (350°F/gas 4). You could replace the paprika with other spices, according to taste.

Frite sauce

POLENTA FRITES

300 ML (1¼ CUPS) OF MILK

300 ML (1¼ CUPS) OF WATER

150 G (GENEROUS ¾ CUP) OF POLENTA (CORNMEAL)

1 TBSP OF PARMESAN, GRATED

1 TBSP OF MELTED BUTTER

2 LITRES (8½ CUPS) OF COOKING OIL

1 TSP OF TABLE SALT

½ TSP OF SEA SALT CRYSTALS

● **Bring the milk** and water to the boil together. Sprinkle in the polenta (cornmeal) and allow to cook for 10 minutes, stirring until it thickens. Add the Parmesan and melted butter. Salt generously and stir well.

● **Spread the polenta (cornmeal)** out on a flat dish, in an even layer about 2 cm or 3 cm (¾ in to 1¼ in) thick and leave to cool. Then put it in the fridge for one hour.

● **Heat** the fryer to 170°C (338°F).

● **Cut the polenta (cornmeal)** into sticks about 10 cm (4 in) long.

● **Put the sticks** carefully into the frying basket, using tongs. Space them out well.

● **Lower the basket** and fry for 2 minutes. Lift out the basket, let the frites drain, then place them carefully on a large plate covered with kitchen paper. Remove the paper.

● **Sprinkle** lightly with sea salt and eat while nice and hot.

THESE GO WELL WITH :
    FRITE SAUCE
    HOMEMADE KETCHUP
    TANGY TOMATO SAUCE
    BÉARNAISE SAUCE

> **TOP TIP...**
>
> This recipe can also be made as a dessert. Simply replace the Parmesan and the salt with caster (superfine) sugar. Serve sprinkled with icing (confectioner's) sugar or cocoa powder.

Tangy tomato sauce

Fries

FETA FRITES

4   5   3

400 G (14 OZ) OF FETA CHEESE (OR ANOTHER SHEEP'S CHEESE)

2 TBSP OF FLOUR

2 EGGS

3 TBSP OF DRIED BREADCRUMBS

2 LITRES (8½ CUPS) OF COOKING OIL

TABLE SALT

FRESHLY GROUND BLACK PEPPER

● **Leave the feta** in the fridge until the last minute so that it remains nice and firm.

● **Cut the feta** into sticks about 1 cm (½ in) wide.

● **Put the flour** into a dish, beat the eggs in a second dish and mix the breadcrumbs with a pinch of salt and a twist of pepper, in a third dish.

● **Heat the fryer** to 170°C (338°F). Put the sticks of feta into each dish in sequence, coating them with the flour, then the eggs and finally the breadcrumbs.

● **Place** them carefully in the basket and lower into the oil. Cook for 3 minutes.

● **Drain** the feta frites and tip them onto a large plate covered with kitchen paper. Remove the paper and season if necessary.

● **Serve** immediately.

THESE GO WELL WITH :
　　FRESH HERB SAUCE
　　SOY SAUCE
　　TANGY TOMATO SAUCE
　　ONION SAUCE

TOP TIP...

For an extra crispy coating, add a few crushed up cornflakes (use a rolling pin or your processor to crush them). Add them to the breadcrumbs before coating the feta.

Tangy tomato sauce

FRITA FETES

CARROT FRITES

4 10 5

1 KG (2.2 LB) OF CARROTS

2 LITRES (8½ CUPS) OF COOKiNG OiL

SEA SALT CRYSTALS

◉ **Heat** the fryer to 170°C (338°F).

◉ **Peel and wash** the carrots. Rinse them well and dry carefully with a clean, dry cloth.

◉ **Cut the carrots** into long, thick pieces using a kitchen knife, then cut them again to make fine sticks about 1 cm (½ in) wide.

◉ **Rinse the carrots** once more and dry carefully. If you are using small young carrots, you could fry them whole with their greens on.

◉ **Tip the carrot sticks** into the basket and cook for 5 minutes, keeping a close watch. Lift out the basket and drain the frites on a plate lined with kitchen paper. Remove the paper.

◉ **Salt** generously and enjoy whilst nice and hot.

THESE GO WELL WiTH :
   TARTAR SAUCE
   CURRY SAUCE
   FRESH HERB SAUCE
   BLUE CHEESE SAUCE

> ### TOP TiP...
>
> If the carrots are too firm for your taste, try blanching them first. Drop them into boiling water for 5 minutes. You will need to keep a careful eye on the frying time; 3 or 4 minutes should be enough.

Curry sauce

AUBERGINE (EGGPLANT) FRITES

1 KG (2.2 LB) OF AUBERGINES (EGGPLANTS)

FRESHLY-SQUEEZED JUICE OF 1 LEMON

2 EGGS

2 TBSP OF FLOUR

3 TBSP OF DRIED BREADCRUMBS

2 TBSP OF PARMESAN, GRATED

A PINCH OF GARLIC POWDER

½ TSP OF TOMATO POWDER

2 LITRES (8½ CUPS) OF COOKING OIL

SEA SALT CRYSTALS

FRESHLY GROUND BLACK PEPPER

● **Heat** the fryer to 170°C (338°F).

● **Peel and wash** the aubergines (eggplants).

● **Cut large slices** from the length of the aubergines (eggplants) with a kitchen knife, then cut the slices into sticks about 10 cm (4 in) long.

● **Pour the lemon juice** into a dish and let the aubergine (eggplant) sticks soak briefly. This will stop them turning brown.

● **Beat the eggs** in a bowl, put the flour into another bowl and use a third bowl for the breadcrumbs, garlic and tomato powder. Add a few salt crystals and a twist of ground pepper to each dish.

● **Dip** the aubergine (eggplant) pieces into the flour, then the eggs and finally the breadcrumb mixture. Place each one carefully in the frying basket.

● **Fry** for 3 minutes, watching closely.

● **Remove** the aubergine (eggplant) frites from the fryer and drain on kitchen paper. Then transfer to a serving dish. Season as necessary and serve piping hot.

THESE GO WELL WITH :
HOMEMADE KETCHUP
ONION SAUCE
FRESH HERB SAUCE
FRITE SAUCE

TOP TIP...

You can find tomato powder in health food stores or from specialist internet sites. Try also carrot, leek or black radish powder, which have a very concentrated flavour and act as natural flavour enhancers in your cooking. These powders are made from dehydrated vegetables that are then ground into a powder.

Frite sauce

COURGETTE (ZUCCHINI), PARMESAN AND POPPY SEED FRITES

1 KG (2.2 LB) OF COURGETTES (ZUCCHINI)

2 EGGS

2 TBSP OF FLOUR

3 TBSP OF DRIED BREADCRUMBS

2 TBSP OF PARMESAN, GRATED

1 TSP OF POPPY SEEDS

2 LITRES (8½ CUPS) OF COOKING OIL

TABLE SALT

FRESHLY GROUND BLACK PEPPER

● **Heat** the fryer to 170°C (338°F).

● **Wash** the courgettes (zucchini) well and dry them carefully with a clean, dry cloth.

● **Cut the courgettes** (zucchini) lengthways into large slices, then cut them again into fairly thin sticks about 10 cm (4 in) long.

● **Beat the eggs** in a bowl, put the flour into a second bowl and mix the breadcrumbs, Parmesan and poppy seeds in a third. Add salt and pepper to all three bowls.

● **Dip** the courgette (zucchini) pieces first in the flour, then in the eggs and finally in the breadcrumb mixture. Place each one carefully in the frying basket.

● **Fry** for 5 minutes, keeping a close eye on them.

● **Remove the courgettes** (zucchini) frites from the fryer. Salt generously and enjoy whilst still hot.

THESE GO WELL WITH :
   HOMEMADE KETCHUP
   TARTAR SAUCE
   CURRY SAUCE
   BLUE CHEESE SAUCE

TOP TIP...

If you prefer, you can peel the courgettes (zucchini) before slicing them. Choose small, firm courgettes (zucchini) as these will be sweeter. Add a pinch of curry powder to the Parmesan for a nice golden finish.

Tartar sauce

ASPARAGUS FRITES

2   10   3

1 BUNCH OF WHITE ASPARAGUS

1 TBSP OF FLOUR

2 TBSP OF DRIED BREADCRUMBS.

1 TSP OF GOMASIO

(A MIXTURE OF SESAME SEEDS AND SALT)

1 EGG

2 LITRES (8¼ CUPS) OF COOKING OIL

SEA SALT CRYSTALS

FRESHLY GROUND BLACK PEPPER

● **Heat** the fryer to 170°C (338°F).

● **Wash and peel** the asparagus carefully, from just below the tip to the base. Cut away the toughest part of the stem.

● **Put the flour** into a long dish. Mix the breadcrumbs with the gomasio in a second dish, and beat the egg in a third dish.

● **Dip the asparagus pieces** one at a time into the flour, then the egg and finally into the breadcrumb mixture.

● **Place** each one carefully in the frying basket using tongs. Take care not to break the tips.

● **Lower the basket** and fry for 3 minutes keeping a close eye on them. Remove the asparagus and leave to drain on kitchen paper.

● **Serve immediately** after seasoning, if necessary.

THESE GO WELL WITH :
    FRITE SAUCE
    TARTAR SAUCE
    FRESH HERB SAUCE
    BLUE CHEESE SAUCE
    BÉARNAISE SAUCE

TOP TIP...

If following the directions above, the asparagus will be quite crunchy. If you prefer it to be slightly more tender, cook for a few minutes longer, but lower the temperature of your fryer to 150 °C or 160 °C (302°F or 320°F) so that the coating doesn't brown too fast. If you prefer, you could blanch them quickly (3 or 4 minutes) in boiling water before frying. If you do this, be sure to dry them thoroughly before frying.

Blue cheese sauce

KOHLRABI
FRITES

butte

Sweet potato frites

BLACK RADISH FRITES

TURNIP FRITES

PARSNI

PANISSE
FRITES

BE

nut squash frites

creative
frites

COMTÉ CHEESE FRÏ

FRITES

SALSIFY FRITES

pumpkin frites

TROOT (BEET) FRITES

TURNIP FRITES

- **Preheat** the oven to 180°C (350°F/gas 4).

- **Peel the turnips** with a small knife or vegetable peeler.

- **Wash them** in cold water and cut into thick slices. Cut these into reasonably chunky sticks.

- **Put the sticks** into a large bowl, pour over the grapeseed oil and sprinkle with the salt, pepper and Chinese five spice. Be careful not to use more than 3 tablespoons of the grapeseed oil because turnips have a porous flesh that absorbs liquid easily.

- **Put the turnip sticks** on a baking sheet lined with greaseproof (parchment) paper.

- **Bake in the oven** for 15 minutes. Keep an eye on them and turn quickly halfway through cooking time.

- **Serve** immediately.

THESE GO WELL WITH :
    SOY SAUCE
    HOMEMADE KETCHUP
    FRITE SAUCE
    AIOLI

3 LARGE TURNIPS

3 TBSP OF GRAPESEED OIL

½ TSP OF CHINESE FIVE SPICE

SEA SALT CRYSTALS

FRESHLY GROUND BLACK PEPPER

PARSNIP FRITES

- **Peel and wash the parsnips.** Dry them thoroughly with a clean, dry cloth.

- **Slice the parsnips** into long, thick pieces then cut them into 10-cm (4-in) long sticks.

- **Heat** the fryer to 180°C (356°F). Put the parsnip pieces in the basket and fry for 8 to 10 minutes.

- **Tip out onto a plate** lined with kitchen paper and leave for a few minutes to drain. Then remove the paper.

- **Add seasoning** and sprinkle over the Chinese five spice. Serve immediately.

THESE GO WELL WITH :
    FRITE SAUCE
    BLUE CHEESE SAUCE
    CURRY SAUCE
    BÉARNAISE SAUCE

5 OR 6 MEDIUM-SIZED PARSNIPS

1 TSP OF CHINESE FIVE SPICE

2 LITRES (8½ CUPS) OF COOKING OIL

TABLE SALT

FRESHLY GROUND BLACK PEPPER

Turnip frites

Frite sauce

COMTÉ CHEESE FRITES

● **Remove** the rind from the Comté and cut the cheese into 1-cm (½-in) wide sticks.

● **Put the flour** into one dish, beat the egg in another dish and mix the breadcrumbs with a little salt and ground pepper in a third.

● **Heat** the fryer to 170°C (338°F). Dip each stick of cheese in the flour, and then the egg and finally the breadcrumbs.

● **Place the cheese sticks** carefully in the basket and fry for 3 minutes.

● **Drain** and tip into a large bowl lined with kitchen paper.

● **Serve** straightaway.

THESE GO WELL WITH :
    FRESH HERB SAUCE
    SOY SAUCE
    ONION SAUCE

1 THICK PIECE OF COMTÉ CHEESE (ABOUT 250 G/ 8 OZ)

2 TBSP OF FLOUR

1 EGG

1 TBSP OF DRIED BREADCRUMBS

2 LITRES (8½ CUPS) OF COOKING OIL

TABLE SALT

FRESHLY GROUND BLACK PEPPER

PUMPKIN FRITES

● **Preheat** the oven to 190°C (375°F/gas 5).

● **Cut the pumpkin** into quarters and remove the rind with a knife. Slice into large pieces that you can then trim to make 10-cm (4-in) long sticks.

● **Place the sticks** in a large bowl, pour over the olive oil and mix well.

● **Put the oiled pumpkin sticks** into a freezer bag with the garlic, ginger, breadcrumbs, salt and pepper and shake thoroughly so that each piece is completely coated with the mixture.

● **Line a baking sheet** with greaseproof (parchment) paper and spread the frites out on it, making sure they don't overlap.

● **Cook** in the centre of the oven for 20 minutes, keeping a close eye on them as they cook.

● **Preheat the grill (broiler)** and 3 minutes before the end of the cooking time move the baking sheet underneath so that the frites turn golden. Take care not to burn them. As soon as they have browned, remove them from the grill (broiler).

● **Season** if necessary and enjoy straightaway.

THESE GO WELL WITH :
    BARBECUE SAUCE
    SOY SAUCE
    FRITE SAUCE

1 PUMPKIN

½ TSP OF GARLIC POWDER

1 ½ TSP OF GROUND GINGER

2 TBSP OF DRIED BREADCRUMBS

5 TBSP OF OLIVE OIL

TABLE SALT

FRESHLY GROUND BLACK PEPPER

Fresh herb sauce

Comté cheese frites

SWEET POTATO AND CUMIN FRITES

3 LARGE SWEET POTATOES

1 TSP OF GROUND CUMiN

2 LiTRES (8½ CUPS) OF COOKiNG OiL

SEA SALT CRYSTALS

FRESHLY GROUND BLACK PEPPER

● **Peel** the sweet potatoes and wash them under cold water.

● **Cut the potatoes** into large slices using a kitchen knife and then trim them to make fat sticks. Rinse again and dry thoroughly with a clean, dry cloth.

● **Heat** the fryer to 180°C (356°F).

● **Put the sweet potato pieces** in the frying basket and fry for 7 minutes. Don't overfill the basket. It's better to fry in several batches as this ensures the frites cook evenly.

● **Lift the basket** and check that the frites are golden. If necessary, put them back for 2 or 3 minutes until they are nice and crisp.

● **Tip the frites** out into a large bowl lined with kitchen paper and leave to drain. Remove the paper.

● **Sprinkle with cumin**, mix well and then add the sea salt and fresh pepper.

● **Serve** straightaway.

THESE GO WELL WiTH :
SOY SAUCE
BARBECUE SAUCE
CURRY SAUCE

> **TOP TiP...**
>
> Sweet potatoes are naturally sweet and therefore work well as a main dish or as a dessert (see pages 104-105). Don't hesitate to mix them with sharp flavours for a sweet and sour dish: the night before, you could put the sweet potatoes in a sealed container with a piece of fresh, peeled ginger root. This will infuse the sweet potato with the ginger flavour quite naturally. You could also try soaking them in a sauce of slightly reduced balsamic vinegar.

Barbecue sauce

BEETROOT (BEET) FRITES

3 LARGE RED BEETROOTS (BEETS), RAW

2 LITRES (8½ CUPS) OF COOKING OIL

SEA SALT CRYSTALS

FRESHLY GROUND BLACK PEPPER

- **Rinse** the beetroots (beets) quickly in water. Top and tail them and remove the skin with a vegetable peeler.

- **Cut into thick slices** and trim to make frites, about 1.5 cm (⅝ in) thick.

- **Dry well** with kitchen paper, removing as much moisture as possible. (Take care: beetroot (beet) will stain both your hands and your clothes).

- **Heat** the fryer to 170°C (338°F), then put the beetroot (beet) pieces into the basket.

- **Lower the basket** into the fryer and fry the beetroot (beet) for 8 minutes.

- **Remove the basket** and leave the beetroot (beet) frites to drain. Pierce them with a fork to check they are cooked. They should be slightly firm to the touch.

- **Tip** out onto a plate lined with kitchen paper. Remove the paper.

- **Sprinkle** immediately with salt and pepper and eat while still hot.

THESE GO WELL WITH :
   CURRY SAUCE
   FRITE SAUCE
   TANGY TOMATO SAUCE

TOP TIP...

Coat the vegetable sticks in breadcrumbs: beat one egg in a bowl and mix dried breadcrumbs with 1 teaspoon of gomasio (a mix of sesame seeds and sea salt) in another bowl. Dip the chopped beetroot (beet) sticks into the egg and then into the breadcrumb mixture and fry as indicated in the recipe above. Adjust the seasoning before serving these deliciously crispy frites.

Curry sauce

CELERIAC FRITES

1 LARGE BULB OF CELERIAC
2 LITRES (8¼ CUPS) OF COOKING OIL
SEA SALT CRYSTALS
FRESHLY GROUND BLACK PEPPER
DRIED MIXED HERBS (OPTIONAL)

● **Heat** the fryer to 180°C (356°F).

● **Peel the celeriac.** Hold it firmly on the chopping board with one hand and use a knife to slice off the skin from top to bottom with the other. Trim off enough to get rid of the tough outer layer.

● **Cut large slices of celeriac** and then trim into fairly large sticks (about 1 cm/½ in thick).

● **Rinse the celeriac sticks** and blanch them in boiling water for 5 minutes. Dry carefully.

● **Put the sticks** into the frying basket and fry for 5 minutes, keeping a close eye on them. Leave them to drain on a plate lined with kitchen paper.

● **Serve immediately,** having seasoned as necessary. Sprinkle with dried mixed herbs, if you like.

THESE GO WELL WITH :
    TARTAR SAUCE
    CURRY SAUCE
    BLUE CHEESE SAUCE
    AIOLI

TOP TIP...

Celeriac is a vegetable that turns yellow quickly. If you add a drop of lemon juice and a teaspoon of flour to the cooking water it keeps its colour better.

Tartar sauce

SALSIFY FRITES

4 / 10 / 3

500 G (1 LB) CANNED SALSIFY

2 EGGS

2 TBSP OF FLOUR

3 TBSP OF DRIED BREADCRUMBS

1 TSP OF FLAXSEED

2 LITRES (8¼ CUPS) OF COOKING OIL

SEA SALT CRYSTALS

FRESHLY GROUND BLACK PEPPER

● **Drain the salsify** in a sieve (strainer) for 5 minutes. Dab with kitchen paper to remove any moisture.

● **Heat** the fryer to 170°C (338°F).

● **Beat the eggs** in a dish, put the flour into a second dish and mix the breadcrumbs with the flaxseed in a third. Add salt and pepper to each dish.

● **Dip the salsify** one at a time into the flour, then the eggs and lastly the breadcrumbs.

● **Put in the frying basket** and fry for 3 minutes. Check to see that the coating does not brown too quickly.

● **Tip the salsify** out onto a plate lined with kitchen paper. Remove the paper and serve straightaway after seasoning as necessary.

THESE GO WELL WITH :
   SOY SAUCE
   BARBECUE SAUCE
   CURRY SAUCE
   BÉARNAISE SAUCE

TOP TIP...

I used canned salsify because they are very practical and easy to use. Fresh salsify is hard to come by, but if you do find it, you will need to peel and blanch it first. Flaxseed adds flavour and a nice bite to the breadcrumb coating. You could spice it up even more with a pinch of chilli (chili) powder.

Soy sauce

BLACK RADISH FRITES

◉ **Preheat** the oven to 180°C (350°F/gas 4).

◉ **Peel the radish** and cut into medium thick slices, then into fine sticks. Rinse under cold water and dry thoroughly with a clean, dry cloth.

◉ **Tip the radish pieces** into a large bowl, sprinkle over the olive oil and the oregano and mix well.

◉ **Spread them out** onto a baking sheet lined with greaseproof (parchment) paper, making sure there is space between each one.

◉ **Bake in the preheated oven** for 25 minutes, keeping a close eye on them. The black radish needs quite a long cooking time, but the cooking time may vary slightly depending on your oven.

◉ **Salt generously** and add pepper. Enjoy while hot.

THESE GO WELL WITH :
  FRITE SAUCE
  ONION SAUCE
  SOY SAUCE

3 LARGE BLACK RADISHES

1 TSP OF OREGANO

3 TBSP OF OLIVE OIL

SEA SALT CRYSTALS

FRESHLY GROUND BLACK PEPPER

BUTTERNUT SQUASH FRITES

◉ **Preheat** the oven to 220°C (425°F/gas 7).

◉ **Peel the butternut squash.** The skin can be quite tough and sometimes tricky to remove: hold the squash firmly on the chopping board with one hand and use the other to cut away the skin with a kitchen knife. Work your way around the squash, trying not to remove too much of the flesh with the skin.

◉ **Cut the squash** in two from top to bottom and remove the pith and seeds from the centre. Then slice it lengthways and cut each slice into long sticks. Trim these to make 10-cm (4-in) long pieces.

◉ **Put the butternut pieces** into a large bowl, pour over the avocado oil and mix well.

◉ **Mix together the spices,** salt and pepper and sprinkle over the butternut sticks. Mix again.

◉ **Line a baking sheet** with greaseproof (parchment) paper and spread the sticks out over it, taking care not to let them touch.

◉ **Put the baking sheet** in the middle of the preheated oven for about 20 minutes, keeping a close eye on them.

◉ **Preheat the grill (broiler)** and 3 minutes before the end of the cooking time, move the sheet underneath so that the frites turn brown. Watch closely to make sure they don't burn. As soon as they are nice and golden, remove them from the grill (broiler).

◉ **Tip the frites onto a plate,** season as necessary and serve straightaway.

THESE GO WELL WITH :
  HOMEMADE KETCHUP
  BARBECUE SAUCE
  BLUE CHEESE SAUCE

1 LARGE BUTTERNUT SQUASH (OR 2 SMALL ONES)

5 TBSP OF AVOCADO OIL

1 ½ TSP OF GROUND CORIANDER

1 ½ TSP OF PAPRIKA

TABLE SALT

FRESHLY GROUND BLACK PEPPER

RADIS NOIR

Black radish frites

PANISSE FRITES

2 PANISSES (SEE BELOW)

2 LITRES (8½ CUPS) OF COOKING OIL

2 TSP OF DRIED MIXED HERBS (OPTIONAL)

SEA SALT CRYSTALS

- **Remove** the panisses from their plastic wrapping.

- **Cut into two lengthways** and then trim into medium-sized sticks.

- **Heat** the fryer to 170°C (338°F).

- **Put the panisse sticks** in the basket and lower into the oil for 3 minutes. Watch carefully, they cook very quickly.

- **Serve while nice and hot,** sprinkled with a little sea salt or dried mixed herbs.

THESE GO WELL WITH :
  FRITE SAUCE
  FRESH HERB SAUCE
  ONION SAUCE

> **TOP TIP...**
>
> Panisse is a speciality from Provence made from chickpea paste. You can find it ready prepared, sold vacuum-packed in the fresh produce section of natural food stores. These panisse frites are also good served as a dessert: sprinkle them with brown sugar instead of salt and serve with a fruit coulis. Olive oil is ideal for frying them.

Fresh herb sauce

KOHLRABI FRITES

4 // 10 5

6 SMALL KOHLRABI

2 LITRES (**8¼** CUPS) OF COOKING OIL

SEA SALT CRYSTALS

FRESHLY GROUND BLACK PEPPER

1 TSP OF WHITE SESAME SEEDS

● **Peel the kohlrabi,** taking care to remove a fairly thick layer to make sure you get rid of the fibrous part of the vegetable.

● **Cut into large slices** and then trim into sticks for frying. Wash carefully.

● **Heat the fryer** to 160°C (320°F) and put the kohlrabi sticks into the frying basket.

● **Fry for 5 minutes,** then leave to drain for a few moments on a plate lined with kitchen paper. Remove the paper.

● **Season and sprinkle** over the white sesame seeds. Serve while nice and hot.

THESE GO WELL WITH :
   ONION SAUCE
   SOY SAUCE
   FRITE SAUCE

TOP TIP...

Add a little colour by frying up some sprigs of fresh parsley. Leave them for a few seconds in the hot oil and then let them drain on kitchen paper. Sprinkle them over the kohlrabi frites.

Soy sauce

Banana

SUGARY POTATO

APPLE FRITES

Sweet potato frites

PAIN PE

Pear frit

frites

FRITES

sweet frites

RDU FRITES

SUGARY POTATO
FRITES

1 KG (2.2 LB) OF CHARLOTTE (SALAD) POTATOES

3 TBSP OF OLIVE OIL

2 TBSP OF CASTER (SUPERFINE) SUGAR

1 TBSP OF ROSE SUGAR (SEE TIP)

● **Preheat** the oven to 180°C (350°F/gas 4).

● **Wash** and peel the potatoes, then cut them into thin sticks.

● **Rinse the sticks** several times until the water runs clear, then dry thoroughly with a clean, dry cloth and tip into a large bowl.

● **Pour** over the olive oil and mix well. Add the caster (superfine) sugar and mix again, making sure all the potatoes are well covered.

● **Line** a baking sheet with greaseproof (parchment) paper and spread the potatoes out on it, making sure that they don't overlap.

● **Bake** on the middle shelf of the preheated oven for 30 minutes. Raise the baking sheet to the top shelf for the last 5 minutes of cooking time. The frites are ready when golden but watch them closely to make sure they don't burn.

● **Sprinkle** with a little rose sugar just before serving.

TOP TIP...

Experiment with different types of sugar. There are a huge variety of sugars with different flavours available on the internet: unrefined sugar, brown sugar, vanilla sugar, classic white sugar and then all the coloured and flavoured sugars (strawberry red, blueberry blue, lemon yellow...).

SWEET POTATO AND CANE SUGAR FRITES

4   5   30

3 LARGE SWEET POTATOES

3 TBSP OF OLIVE OIL

2 TBSP OF CASTER (SUPERFINE) SUGAR

- **Preheat** the oven to 180°C (350°F/gas 4).

- **Wash and peel** the sweet potatoes. Cut them into evenly sized sticks.

- **Rinse the sticks,** dry thoroughly and tip into a large bowl. Pour over the olive oil and mix well. Add the sugar and mix again.

- **Line** a baking sheet with greaseproof (parchment) paper and spread the sweet potato sticks out on it, making sure that they don't overlap.

- **Bake** in the middle of the oven for 30 minutes. Move the baking sheet to the top shelf of the oven for the last 5 minutes of cooking time. The frites should be caramelized but watch them closely in case they burn.

- **Sprinkle** over a little more sugar just before serving.

> **TOP TIP...**
>
> If you have a very sweet tooth and enjoy rich desserts, try these frites piled up on a plate, topped with condensed milk or maple syrup. You could even add whipped cream.

BANANA AND BROWN SUGAR FRITES

4 FIRM BANANAS

3 TBSP OF NATURAL BROWN SUGAR

◉ **Preheat** the oven to 150°C (300°F/gas 2).

◉ **Peel** the bananas and cut in half lengthways, then cut them into 10-cm (4-in) long sticks.

◉ **Dip** each stick into the sugar, making sure it is completely coated.

◉ **Spread the banana** pieces out onto a baking sheet lined with greaseproof (parchment) paper, making sure they don't overlap.

◉ **Bake** on a high shelf in the oven for no more than 5 minutes. Keep a close eye on the frites to make sure they don't burn. Be aware that banana goes soft very quickly.

◉ **Put the banana** frites carefully on a wooden board or a plate and let them cool. The caramelized sugar will harden slightly, making them nice and crunchy.

◉ **Eat** while still warm with a fork.

> **TOP TIP...**
>
> Natural brown sugar is an unrefined cane sugar that still contains molasses. It is dark in colour and has a slight taste of licorice and vanilla.

APPLE FRITES

4 GRANNY SMITH APPLES

FRESHLY-SQUEEZED JUICE OF ½ A LEMON

25 G (1 TBSP) OF SALTED BUTTER

3 TBSP OF NATURAL BROWN SUGAR

- **Preheat** the oven to 190°C (375°F/gas 5).

- **Peel the apples** and cut them into quarters. Remove the core and seeds and cut into fat sticks.

- **Put the apple pieces** into a large bowl and pour over the lemon juice. Stir to make sure the apple is well covered with lemon juice – this will prevent it turning brown.

- **Melt the butter** and pour it over the apple sticks. Add the brown sugar and mix well again.

- **Put the apples** on a baking sheet lined with greaseproof (parchment) paper, making sure that they don't overlap.

- **Bake** on a high shelf in the oven for 10 minutes. The apple frites will caramelize on the outside. Watch carefully to make sure that they don't burn and that they don't go too soft (oven temperatures and cooking times may vary).

- **Serve warm** and sprinkle over a little extra sugar, if you wish.

TOP TIP...

You could serve these apple frites with chocolate sauce: melt a little dark chocolate with a dash of whipping cream either in the microwave or in a bain-marie. Add a drop of vanilla extract and a pinch of ground cinnamon. Dip your frites in the sauce and enjoy. You can also make this recipe with unpeeled apples.

PEAR FRITES

4 CONFERENCE PEARS, NOT TOO RIPE

FRESHLY-SQUEEZED JUICE OF ½ A LEMON

1 EGG

3 TBSP OF PRALINE (SEE TIP)

● **Preheat** the oven to 170°C (325°F/gas 3).

● **Peel the pears** and cut them in half. Remove the core and the seeds and cut them into fairly fat sticks. Sprinkle over the lemon juice so that they don't turn brown.

● **Beat the egg** in a dish. If the praline isn't already ground, put it on a board, cover with cling film (plastic wrap), and crush with a rolling pin until it is a fine powder. Put this in a separate dish.

● **Dip the sticks** of pear into the egg and then into the praline powder.

● **Spread out the pear sticks** on a baking sheet lined with greaseproof (parchment) paper.

● **Bake** in the middle of the oven for 10 minutes, moving the baking sheet to the top shelf of the oven for the last 3 minutes. Watch closely so that they don't burn.

● **Eat while warm,** with your fingers or with a fork.

TOP TIP...

Praline is a mixture of sugar, hazelnuts and almonds, that you can find ready-made in supermarkets. But it is also easy to make yourself: mix an equal amount of sugar with ground hazelnuts and ground almonds (for 100 g/½ cup of sugar use 50 g/½ cup each of ground hazelnuts and ground almonds). The mixture will keep for several weeks in an airtight container.

PAIN PERDU FRITES

4 10 3

8 SLICES OF SLIGHTLY STALE BREAD

2 LITRES (8½ CUPS) OF COOKING OIL

2 EGGS

1 TSP OF AGAVE SYRUP

2 TBSP OF FLOUR

2 TBSP OF CASTER (SUPERFINE) SUGAR

3 TBSP OF NATURAL BROWN SUGAR

- **Remove** the crusts and cut the slices of bread into sticks.
- **Heat** the fryer to 180°C (356°F).
- **Beat the eggs** in a dish and add the agave syrup.
- **Mix the flour** and caster (superfine) sugar together in a second dish.
- **Dip each bread stick** into the egg-syrup mix and then into the flour–sugar mix, so that the bread is completely coated.
- **Put the coated sticks** carefully in the frying basket and then lower into the oil for 3 minutes.
- **Remove** the pain perdu frites and place them on kitchen paper to get rid of any excess oil.
- **Serve** them straightaway, sprinkled with a little natural brown sugar.

TOP TIP...

Experiment with the flavour of your pain perdu frites: add a teaspoon of Grand Marnier or natural vanilla extract to the beaten egg. You could also sprinkle ground cinnamon, cocoa powder or icing (confectioner's) sugar over them just before serving.

parsley

bouquet garni

ONION SAUCE

onion

sweet onion

Fresh herb sauce

poppy seeds

garlic

cloves

aioli

milk

tarragon

shallots

BÉARNAISE SAUCE

soy sauce

curry sauce

mixed spice

curry

honey

Barbeque sauce

mustard

Sauces

tomatoes

freshly ground pepper

MOUT

caster (superfine) sugar

HOMEMADE KETCHUP

flour

olive oil

blue cheese

FRITE SAUCE

Miel
BZZZ

1 TBSP OF OLIVE OIL

2 ONIONS, FINELY CHOPPED

1 CLOVE OF GARLIC, FINELY CHOPPED

3 CLOVES (GROUND TO A POWDER)

1 TSP OF MIXED SPICE

1 KG (2.2 LB) OF TOMATOES, SKINNED

6 TBSP OF CASTER (SUPERFINE) SUGAR

200 ML (GENEROUS ¾ CUP) OF HONEY (OR CIDER) VINEGAR

1 TSP OF HONEY

A PINCH OF PAPRIKA

1 TSP OF TOMATO PURÉE (PASTE)

TABLE SALT

FRESHLY GROUND BLACK PEPPER

HOMEMADE KETCHUP

● **Heat the oil** in a frying pan (skillet) and add the onions, garlic, ground cloves, mixed spice and tomatoes.

● **Leave to simmer** on a low heat for 45 minutes. Halfway through the cooking time, crush the tomatoes with a wooden spoon to break them down.

● **Add the sugar,** vinegar, honey, paprika and tomato purée (paste).

● **Leave the sauce to thicken** for about 1½ hours. Remove from the heat, adjust the seasoning and put aside to cool.

● **Put the sauce** through a fine sieve to get rid of the tomato seeds. Store in the fridge for at least 2 or 3 days to chill well before serving.

TOP TIP...

The more fragrant the ketchup, the better. So don't hesitate to experiment with different herbs and spices: cumin, licorice, cinnamon, ginger, basil, will all add to the flavour of your ketchup.

1 TBSP OF OLIVE OIL

1 ONION, FINELY CHOPPED

1 CLOVE OF GARLIC, FINELY CHOPPED

3 TBSP OF KETCHUP

1 TSP OF TOMATO PUREÉ (PASTE)

1 TSP OF WORCESTERSHIRE SAUCE
(OR BROWN SAUCE)

2 TSP OF HONEY

2 TBSP OF PAPRIKA

TABLE SALT

FRESHLY GROUND BLACK PEPPER

BARBECUE SAUCE

● **Heat the olive oil** in a frying pan (skillet) and fry the onion and garlic over a gentle heat. Add salt and pepper and cook gently, taking care not to let the mixture brown.

● **Add** the remaining ingredients and leave to cook slowly, stirring regularly until the sauce thickens.

● **Add** a little water to thin the sauce if it is too thick.

● **Enjoy** this sauce either hot or cold.

> **TOP TIP...**
>
> In place of brown sauce or Worcestershire sauce, you could just add one teaspoon of malt vinegar and one teaspoon of molasses to the recipe.

2 EGG YOLKS

2 HEAPED TSP OF FRENCH MUSTARD

A DROP OF WHITE WINE (OR CIDER) VINEGAR

½ TSP OF HONEY

300 ML (1¼ CUPS) OF SUNFLOWER OIL

TABLE SALT

FRESHLY GROUND BLACK PEPPER

FRITE SAUCE

● **Choose a bowl** that is not too wide and reasonably tall. This will help make a stiff mayonnaise.

● **Add** the egg yolks, mustard, vinegar, salt, pepper and honey.

● **Make your mayonnaise** using a wire whisk and pouring in the sunflower oil in a very slow trickle. Keep whisking constantly and don't hesitate to add a little mustard if the consistency seems too liquid. If you do this, you will need to add the same amount of oil.

● **Stop whisking** once the consistency is stiff enough. Season as necessary.

● **Keep in the fridge** and serve this sauce well chilled.

TOP TIP...

French mustard is an aromatic mustard that is slightly sweet and not as strong as English mustard. You should find it easily in the supermarket or you could make your own by adding a little brown sugar powder, ground coriander or a pinch of turmeric to ordinary mustard.

2 SHALLOTS, FINELY CHOPPED

100 ML (SCANT ½ CUP) OF WHITE WINE VINEGAR

6 TBSP OF CHOPPED FRESH TARRAGON

200 G (1 STICK/6 TBSP) UNSALTED BUTTER, MELTED

6 EGG YOLKS

2 TSP OF WATER

TABLE SALT

FRESHLY GROUND BLACK PEPPER

BÉARNAISE SAUCE

● **Put the shallots** in a saucepan with the vinegar, half the tarragon and a little freshly ground pepper.

● **Heat slowly** for 10 minutes until the vinegar has evaporated.

● **Remove the saucepan** from the heat and add the egg yolks and the water. Whisk the mixture quickly and then let it thicken over a bain-marie (or a very low heat) stirring constantly.

● **Remove from the heat** and trickle in the melted butter a little at a time, whisking constantly.

● **Pour the sauce** into a serving bowl and add the remaining tarragon, the salt and pepper.

● **Serve** this sauce warm or cold.

> ### TOP TIP...
>
> You can make a lighter Béarnaise sauce by replacing the butter with crème fraiche (soured cream) or natural yogurt, or with a teaspoon of cornflour (cornstarch) dissolved in a little water. Season generously as cornflour (cornstarch) tends to dull other flavours.

TARTAR SAUCE

🔵 **Put the egg yolks** in a high-sided bowl. Add the mustard, vinegar, salt and pepper.

🔵 **Make the mayonnaise** using a wire whisk and slowly adding the sunflower oil in a very slow trickle. Keep whisking constantly until it has a good, stiff consistency.

🔵 Mix the chopped spring onion (scallion), capers, gherkins and herbs into the mayonnaise. Check the seasoning and adjust as necessary.

🔵 **Serve** well chilled.

2 EGG YOLKS

1 HEAPED TBSP OF STRONG MUSTARD

A DASH OF WINE VINEGAR

200 ML (GENEROUS ¾ CUP) OF SUNFLOWER OIL

1 SPRING ONION (SCALLION), FINELY CHOPPED

1 TBSP OF CAPERS, FINELY CHOPPED

10 GHERKINS, FINELY CHOPPED

1 SMALL BUNCH OF FRESH PARSLEY, CHERVIL, TARRAGON AND CHIVES, FINELY CHOPPED

TABLE SALT

FRESHLY GROUND BLACK PEPPER

AIOLI

🔵 **Crush the garlic cloves.** Put the egg yolks into a high-sided bowl and add the crushed garlic, mustard, vinegar, salt and pepper.

🔵 **Make your mayonnaise** using a wire whisk and adding the sunflower oil in a very slow trickle. Keep whisking constantly until the sauce has a good, stiff consistency.

🔵 **Check** the seasoning and adjust as necessary.

🔵 **Serve** well chilled.

5 CLOVES OF GARLIC

2 EGG YOLKS

1 HEAPED TBSP OF STRONG MUSTARD

A DASH OF WINE VINEGAR

200 ML (GENEROUS ¾ CUP) OF SUNFLOWER OIL

TABLE SALT

FRESHLY GROUND BLACK PEPPER

50 G (3½ TBSP) OF BUTTER

50 G (6 TBSP) OF FLOUR

400 ML (1¾ CUPS) OF MILK

150 G (7 OZ) BLUE CHEESE

TABLE SALT

FRESHLY GROUND BLACK PEPPER

BLUE CHEESE SAUCE

● **Melt the butter** in a saucepan over a low heat. Sift over the flour slowly and stir. Let it brown slightly.

● **Pour in the milk** a little at a time, stirring constantly. Then crumble the blue cheese and add it, still stirring, until the cheese melts. Keep stirring so that the sauce thickens.

● **Add salt and pepper,** then serve the sauce nice and hot.

TOP TIP...

This cheese sauce, made from a béchamel base, is traditionally made with mimolette in Belgium. The same recipe can be used to make macaroni cheese (mac and cheese); don't hesitate to replace the blue cheese with Cheddar, or even with Comté or camembert.

2 EGG YOLKS

1 HEAPED TBSP OF STRONG MUSTARD

A DASH OF WHITE WINE VINEGAR

APPROX. 200 ML (GENEROUS ¾ CUP) OF SUNFLOWER OIL

1 TSP OF CURRY POWDER

TABLE SALT

FRESHLY GROUND BLACK PEPPER

CURRY SAUCE

● **Put the egg yolks** and the mustard in a high-sided bowl. Add the vinegar, salt and pepper.

● **Make your mayonnaise** with a wire whisk, adding the sunflower oil in a very slow trickle. Keep whisking constantly until the mayonnaise has a good, stiff consistency.

● **Add the curry powder** and whisk the mayonnaise one last time. Season with salt and pepper, if necessary, and serve chilled.

TOP TIP...

You could make a lighter version of this sauce by replacing the mayonnaise with crème fraiche (soured cream). You could also try a more exotic, warm version by mixing 250 ml (1 cup) of crème fraiche (soured cream) with 2 tablespoons of coconut milk over a low heat for 10 minutes.

TANGY TOMATO **SAUCE**

- **Fry the onions,** shallots and garlic very lightly in the olive oil, stirring constantly so that they don't brown.

- **Drop the tomatoes** in boiling water and skin them. Chop them up small and add to the frying pan. Pour over the white wine and the cognac and add the bouquet garni. Stir and then sprinkle over the paprika.

- **Season generously** with salt and pepper and then transfer the mixture to a hand-held blender or food processor. Blend until the mixture is more-or-less smooth but still with a little texture.

- **Return to the pan** and reheat for a few minutes. Add the flour diluted in a little hot water and turn up the heat to allow the sauce to thicken. Then remove the pan from the heat.

- **Serve** the sauce piping hot.

3 TBSP OF OLIVE OIL
3 ONIONS, FINELY CHOPPED
2 SHALLOTS, FINELY CHOPPED
2 CLOVES OF GARLIC, FINELY CHOPPED
4 TOMATOES
1 GLASS OF WHITE WINE
2 TBSP OF COGNAC
1 BOUQUET GARNI
1 TSP OF PAPRIKA
1 TBSP OF FLOUR
TABLE SALT
FRESHLY GROUND BLACK PEPPER

ONION **SAUCE**

- **Melt the butter** in a saucepan over a low heat. Add the finely chopped onion and the vinegar. Season with salt and pepper and brown lightly.

- **Sprinkle over the flour** and then add the stock. Keep stirring over a low heat until the sauce thickens.

- **Add the sugar** and stir again.

- **Season** as necessary. Serve hot.

40 G (3 TBSP) OF UNSALTED BUTTER
5 ONIONS, FINELY CHOPPED
1 TSP OF VINEGAR
2 TBSP OF FLOUR
300 ML (1¼ CUPS) OF CHICKEN STOCK
1 TBSP OF CASTER (SUPERFINE) SUGAR
TABLE SALT
FRESHLY GROUND BLACK PEPPER

3 TBSP OF BLACK RICE VINEGAR
2 TBSP OF SOY SAUCE
½ TSP SESAME OIL
HOT RED PEPPER (CHILI) SAUCE

SOY SAUCE

- **Pour** the black rice vinegar into a bowl.
- **Add the soy sauce** and the sesame oil.
- **Stir well** to bind the sauce.
- **Add a drop of** hot red pepper (chili) sauce, if you want to spice it up a little.

> **TOP TIP...**
>
> Black rice vinegar is a traditional ingredient in Chinese sauces and marinades. You can also find white rice vinegar in supermarkets, which has a milder flavour. Use this with a spoonful of sugar instead of the hot red pepper (chili) for a sweeter sauce.

2 EGG YOLKS

1 HEAPED TBSP OF STRONG MUSTARD

A DASH OF WHITE WINE (OR CIDER) VINEGAR

200 ML (GENEROUS ¾ CUP) OF SUNFLOWER OIL

½ A BUNCH OF FRESH PARSLEY

½ A BUNCH OF FRESH CHIVES

½ A BUNCH OF FRESH CHERVIL

TABLE SALT

FRESHLY GROUND BLACK PEPPER

FRESH HERB SAUCE

- **Choose** a medium-sized bowl with high sides.

- **Beat together the egg yolks** with the mustard, vinegar, salt and pepper.

- **Make your mayonnaise** with a wire whisk, adding the sunflower oil in a very slow trickle, whisking all the time. If it seems too liquid, you could add a little mustard but you will need to add the same amount of oil, too. Stop whisking once the sauce has a good, stiff consistency.

- **Chop up all the herbs,** either with kitchen scissors or with a kitchen knife. Stir them carefully into the mayonnaise. Check the seasoning and adjust as necessary.

- **Keep in the fridge** and serve this sauce well chilled.

TOP TIP...

If you prefer, put the herbs in a food processor and then add them to the mayonnaise to make a green sauce. You could also spice it up a little by adding one small onion, finely chopped.

Index of recipes